S0-ARJ-910

Love Affair

Love Affair

A Prayer Journal

ANDREW M. GREELEY

CROSSROAD • NEW YORK

1992

The Crossroad Publishing Company
370 Lexington Avenue, New York, NY 10017

Printed in the United States of America

Library of Congress Cataloging-in-Publication Data

Greeley, Andrew M., 1928–
Love affair : a prayer journal / Andrew M. Greeley.
p. cm.
ISBN 0-8245-1198-0
1. Greeley, Andrew M., 1928– —Diaries. 2. Catholic Church—Clergy—Diaries. 3. Spiritual journals. I. Title.
BX4705.G6185A3 1992
248.3'2—dc20 92-9482
CIP

Preface

I began the prayer-reflections that eventually became this "journal" when I was writing my parish novel *The Cardinal Virtues*. As I was putting prayers on the lips of the protagonist, Father Laurence O'Toole McAuliffe, I found that I was praying with him, for him, through him. Perhaps, I thought, writing out a prayer on a computer screen might be a useful way to pray — at least a way to focus concentration and attention on praying. I've been working on this journal of prayers for three years. They are the best way to pray I've yet discovered.

I had intended them to be for God only. However, my friend Dan Herr, God be good to him, was convinced that they might prove helpful to others. At his request, I printed out my dialogue with God and said if he wanted to use it for the Thomas More Association, he was welcome to it. My conversations with God were not secret. If anyone else wanted to listen in, they were welcome to do so. However, I refused to revise them because I thought that would be an insult to my dialogue Partner. Dan edited the manuscript, and I refused even to look at it. Nor have I read the published volume (*Year of Grace*) since then, perhaps because of fear of the person I might encounter on the human side of the dialogue. Mike Leach, my publisher at Crossroad who performed the same office as Dan with the second volume, made me glance through it. He eliminated the repetitions, some references to people by name, and a few irrelevancies. Otherwise this account of my love affair with God over the course of a year is the way it happened. As with most love affairs it was an erratic and sometime thing, marked by inconsistency and weakness in one partner and allusiveness in the Other. The affair, however, continues.

And I continue to be astonished that the Lover continues to put up with me. However, that's Her problem.

This then is not *about* prayer, but it is rather a book *of* prayer, weary, discouraged, distracted, extremely imperfect attempts to dialogue with the Beloved Other. If anyone finds help in their own prayer by listening in, they're welcome to do so.

You will hear only one side of the dialogue.

Or maybe you will hear the other side speaking softly if you listen hard enough. As Cardinal Martini points out, we cannot pray without the help of God who prays in us. So maybe you'll hear God praying in me, though I admit I often give Her a hard time.

Lovers don't seem to mind, though.

You will not find in these reflections a diary in the ordinary sense of the word. I don't keep track of what's going on in the world or even in my own life, save perhaps in passing. The two big events of 1991 — the Persian Gulf War and the Fall of the Communist Empire — are discussed only in passing, not because they are unimportant but because they are not pertinent to the dialogue and because God and others can read my columns to find out what I think about political and social issues.

The publisher did ask to reprint in the back of the book an article I wrote for *The Critic,* which summarizes my thinking over the months on the Persian Gulf War. I had no objection to that, though the article itself is not part of my dialogue with the Other in our on-again-off-again love affair.

There are three locales for this affair: Chicago, which is where I live; Tucson, where I am a member of the Department of Sociology at the University of Arizona; and Grand Beach, Michigan, where I am supposed to vacation in the summer, but usually make a poor job of it. I have no idea whether the geography influences my conversations with the Other, but I am grateful to Her for providing such beautiful sacraments of Her love. It seems I get to Dublin pretty often too.

I am conscious of the inadequacy of these prayers. But if you share my sense that I am just a beginner at prayer, perhaps you can learn from my mistakes.

Besides the memory of Dan Herr, I dedicate this book to Martin Phee and his late wife, Kate. Marty is my physician and brought me through the bout of pneumonia and my cancer scare with elegance and skill. Kate was my travel agent, arranged my ill-fated trip to Bangkok, and cancelled my reservation with great good cheer when dizzy with fever I phoned her from LAX. Two weeks later, my heart aching as well as my lungs, I preached at her funeral. May my Lover grant her peace and take care of her family.

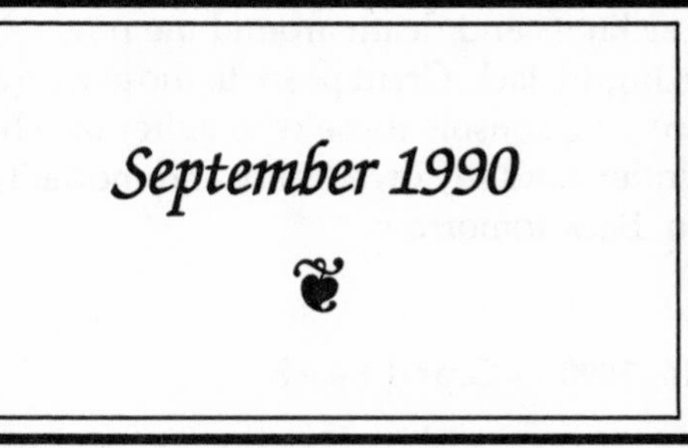

September 1990

September 11, 1990 — Grand Beach, Michigan

My Love,

I came back from New York, both exhausted and exhilarated, and slept only three hours. Will I ever stop being tired? I was so out of it that I said to someone on the phone this morning that it was April instead of September! I must go to Ann Arbor for Barbara's funeral on Thursday, God (You, of course) rest her. I'm so happy that she came into the Church and grateful for the opportunity to celebrate her entry into heaven. But I'm so weary, my Love, and so involved in writing the novel that this frantic traveling is sapping my strength. Please help me through the next few days.

I love You. I'm sorry I'm such a mess. Maybe if I sleep well tonight, which please grant, I'll feel better tomorrow.

September 15, 1990 — Grand Beach

My Love,

Where have the last three days gone? I'm sorry for missing these reflections a couple of times this week. As You know, writing a novel consumes my being and makes me forget about the rest of the world. I'm coming down the homestretch now. I hope You like it because once more, as in *Patience of a Saint*, I'm trying to do a portrait of You. I ask You to help me do it well so that readers will catch a glimpse of Your mercy and love.

So much sickness and death around me now — Barbara, Dan Herr, Ivyone, Ingrid, Jack. Grant peace to those who are gone, help those who are sick, console those who suffer or who worry. And help me to understand my own frailty and mortality.

I love You. Back tomorrow.

September 16, 1990 — Grand Beach

My Love,

A fierce early autumn storm is blowing outside. Summer has burnt away. I thank You for all its graces. I pray for Your help and protection during the busy autumn months. I also pray for the sick and the dead and the suffering and the bereaved. Grant peace and healing, please, to all of them.

The novel is finished! I'll let it sit for most of the week and then go over it again to make sure that it works. It was an extremely ambitious venture for me, if not in genre, then in story and technique — a bigger risk than I've ever taken before

So I'm back on my regular schedule, more or less, and into the transition back to Chicago for which I've organized two relatively free weeks to rearrange my life and write some overdue articles I've promised to friends.

I thank You for helping me to discover that I could write novels — even if it was after the age of fifty-six! To create a story that reveals Your grace in our lives is one of the great joys of my life. When I'm working on them, I can do little else. That's why I must do them here or in Tucson when I can declare a moratorium on most anything else.

I'm sorry if I have been unkind or selfish during these two weeks. Help me to make up for it.

I love You.

September 17, 1990 — Grand Beach

My Love,

I dreamt that I was back at Christ the King parish, my first assignment as a priest. In the dream, the pastor was attacking me for not doing something that was impossible. In fairness, although

I didn't like the man, in reality he did not demand the impossible. So the whole incident had to be a metaphor for the feeling in my unconscious that *I* must do the impossible to make my life worthwhile.

I have no trouble accepting that as a true revelation of my personality. Does not my output suggest someone who works too hard to achieve what seems impossible — however much that achievement may offend some of those he would like to please? And isn't my disappointment when the work is attacked unfairly often just a way of saying, "What more can I do?"

At this stage in my life it would be silly to try to abandon my interests and output. It is also foolish of me to expect praise for it. Finally, it would be a mistake not to try and understand the energies and, if You will, the demons that drive me.

I believe that You approve of what I do and give me credit for it — and that even *You* wish I'd slow down a little, which I'm trying to do. I also believe that You love me.

Finally I believe that You want me to write novels and that You are not upset by the way I write them.

Please take care of, protect, and heal all of the sick people for whom I am praying.

Thank You.

September 18, 1990 — Grand Beach

My Love,

I'm reading the Last Supper discourse in St. John's Gospel. After talking to theologian David Tracy, I'm persuaded that the exegetical/historical approach to John is unhelpful and that the Gospels should be read mystically. This means for a nonmystical person like myself that it must be read meditatively, a verse or two at a time, instead of a paragraph or a chapter at a time.

Yesterday I began the vine and the branches chapter. The theme of the chapter is the intimate relationship between Your son Jesus (and therefore You Yourself) and his followers — the complete dependence of all of us on You.

When I look at the sickness and death around me this month, I realize how true that is on the most fundamental existential level (again I pray for those who are sick; grant that they recover quickly and completely). You thrust us into being and eventually You call us home — that is how the person of faith sees it anyway. One without faith simply sees life as a brief interlude between two oblivions. Our existence is so fragile. We are dependent beings by nature. The *real* issue is whether we depend on Something or Someone, or whether we are suspended by and above nothingness.

That we are branches is clear. The question is whether there is really a vine. But how can You have a vine without branches? How can You have creatures and not have a Creator?

So the question has to be reworded: of what sort is the vine on which we depend? What or who is the Creator who produced us?

The answer in St. John's Gospel is at the core of our tradition: *God is love*. We are suspended by and over Love.

I believe that. I believe that I am utterly dependent on Love, that is to say on You. Please teach me more about that before I return tomorrow.

PRAYER FOR LOVE

O God, who is love, help me to understand my total dependence on Your love. Help me to respond to that love with love of my own. Help me to love others as You love them and as You love me. Help me to see in those who love me the most, hints of You and Your love. Help me to realize that my life makes sense only when I realize that I am adrift in a sea of love. I ask this in the name of Jesus the Lord. Amen.

September 19, 1990 — Grand Beach

My Love,

More about the vine and the branches on this cold and rainy depressing day: first, everything I do depends on my loving union with You. I am not (as one of the prayers I read in a book yesterday suggests) Your "dog." That's the kind of self-degrading talk that discredits the old piety. However, all my work, all my effectiveness as a priest and as a writer are the result of Your strength and love at work within me. I am grateful for the talent and the faith and the energy You have given me. Without those gifts I could do nothing. You are the vine. I am one of Your branches.

Having said this and acknowledged my dependence on You, I must say more. The opposite side of the coin is that with You I can do *everything*. And that's the emphasis which all of us need. We do not need to feel that we are nothing (feeling worthless comes easy most of the time!) — we need rather to feel that we are sustained, supported, protected, and loved by You. That is something! It does not follow that nothing bad will happen in our lives. It does follow that because You are the vine and we are the branches, we will survive and flourish and bear fruit in the long run. Faith is easy when things go well. It is difficult only when life makes it difficult to believe that the vine has not deserted this particular branch. I get in trouble when I get so busy that I don't reflect on the vine parable. Help me to avoid that kind of business and realize my faith.

I am still, to change the subject, struck by the amount of sickness and death in my environment this month. I'm grateful for my own health, though I must realize that eventually it will fail. I also pray again for those who are sick and for those who are mourning. I will try to stay in touch with the latter and do what I can. But healing comes only from You. Heal them, please.

PRAYER ON A GRAY DAY

O God, who charms us by the changing of the days and the seasons, lift up my spirits on this seemingly spiritless day. Grant that my joy over Your love for me may break through the clouds and the darkness and be sunlight for all those around me. I ask this in the name of Jesus the Lord.

Amen.

September 20, 1990 — Grand Beach

My Love,

Just after I wrote that last line, John Sprague [of the Thomas More Association] called with news about Dan Herr [its president], which is not good. They're trying desperately to repair a ruptured blood vessel near his heart. It sounds very problematic to me. Poor brave man! I beg of You to help him. I don't want to lose him if it be Your will. I will drive to Chicago and visit him tonight and tomorrow.

Ingrid is feeling better and seems likely to be able to go home at the end of the week — if they do not have to do thyroid surgery. For which many thanks.

All this sickness and death!

Life is so fragile, so very, very fragile.

Take care of all the sick people I know, I plead with You.

Well, after that opening, I turn with something of a heavy heart to Your wonderful words as spoken through Your son Jesus in St. John's Gospel: "You have not chosen me, I have chosen you."

Immediately the amateur exegete in me wants to ask whether those are really words that Jesus spoke. Well, even if he didn't speak to them, they are an accurate summary of his ministry and teaching experience of God (You!).

The words apply first to the apostles, then, I suppose, to all who do the work of the apostles, such as priests. That was certainly the way they taught me to interpret them in the seminary, and I shouldn't abandon the tradition of spirituality behind them. We priests, through no merit of our own, are chosen in a unique way. (*"But,"* She says...)

But how can anyone deny that they are words spoken to *all Christians* who could not and did not merit the gift of faith? Moreover, must not one extend the meaning of the words to apply to *all those whom You love*? Which is everyone who has ever lived! You choose each one of us to exist the way a lover chooses the beloved. That is the premise, the basic assumption, the first principle of faith — the universality of Your love. You made an inexplicable choice in love that I exist and should be invited to a *love affair* with You!

I believe that last sentence with all my mind. I confess, nonetheless, that it is such an awesome proposition, so beyond my human ability to comprehend or absorb, that I hardly know what to make of it. It ought to dominate my life but, in fact, it does not. I must try my best to lock this thought in my heart and reflect on it often.

I hope that the new novel suggests this theme as powerfully as I can make it. There's no doubt that I believe it, but that's not enough, is it?

Grant that it may permeate and transform my life.

September 21, 1990 — Grand Beach

My Love,

Wow!

That exclamation is occasioned by the film *Flatliners,* which I saw last night, a remarkable exercise in the religious imagination by people who presumably have no particular religious background or theological education. Its theme is that forgiveness is more important than life after death — a statement with which we cannot disagree, especially since Your son Jesus came into the world to assure us that *we* are forgiven. In a universe where the dead and the living can forgive one another (as in this film) life after death is essential. But it is not, the filmmakers seem to say, enough. Life after death without forgiveness wouldn't be worth very much.

I continue to be astonished at the theological sophistication of filmmakers, far above that of the formal theologians. I'm going to use it as a story at Mass tomorrow and on Sunday.

I am grateful that You have forgiven me. I will do my best to forgive in this life so that it won't be necessary in the next, but I'm grateful for the opportunity there too.

Dan Herr is not doing well. They had to do open-heart surgery last night because the more sophisticated procedures didn't work. Please take care of him. Selfishly I do not want to lose him.

A gray day again today with driving rain and the need to get my packing in order. When it's this bad up here the obligation to return to Chicago seems less oppressive. Indeed I'm eager as I always am this time of the year to return to my Chicago life. As much as my life there gets me down sometimes, Chicago is in my bones.

Thank You for the summer.

Help and protect me back in the city I love.

And thank You for the chance to bring my weight under control again. Help me to keep it that way.

September 22, 1990 — Grand Beach

My Love,

I just came in from an hour or so of putting things away for the winter, a melancholy task at best and also an exhausting one.

I am grateful for all the good times of the summer, which seemed to go by too fast as it always does. I am also grateful that I have a wonderful city to return to.

Last night I watched *Two Women*, the film for which Sophia Loren won the Academy Award twenty-nine years ago. She was marvelous, of course, in every way one could imagine. However, the film portrayed again what we Americans have never known, the horrors of war and the random death and destruction suffered by poor and innocent people.

One hears on TV that hundreds thousands of workers are fleeing Iraq and Kuwait — most of them poor people from countries like Egypt, Pakistan, and the Philippines. Whenever evil people create war, the innocent, the harmless, and the powerless suffer. George Bush's intransigent refusal to negotiate is almost as bad as Saddam Hussein's invasion. The magnitude of the suffering is beyond my comprehension.

And there will be much more suffering when the bombs begin to rain.

Protect the poor and the innocent, I beg You, and prevent war!

September 24, 1990 — Chicago

My Love,

If I hate people, Your son Jesus warns in St. John's Gospel, will I not be hating You too? And if others hate me, will they not also hate You?

Fair questions. Why should we be any different from Jesus?

The snide attack on me in a new book on celibacy is so gratuitous and mean-spirited. But what else is new? If I let the author upset me or disrupt my tranquility, I'm giving him power over me that he has no right to have. I will let him win.

The same with the nasty letter I received this morning. Why should I give that person power to diminish my peace of mind?

If people did it to Jesus, who was so much better and more generous and more loving than I can ever hope to be, why should I — a pupil much, much less than the master — expect immunity?

That's the attitude I must strive to maintain, no matter what the provocation or how unjust the charge.

I always hesitate to identify myself with Jesus in these circumstances because my goodness is so incredibly distant from his and because I am reluctant to claim his purity of intent. Yet I at least strive for the same goals and ought to use that Gospel quote as a spiritual lesson — one that works both ways. I must never hate anyone. Neither must I let anyone who hates me spoil my tranquility or peace of mind. Rather I must strive for serenity in this new work year that begins here in Chicago today.

September 25, 1990 — Chicago

My Love,

A lot of imagery is crowding into my head on these September days — the film on the Civil War, *Good Fellas*, last night; *Flatliners*, last week. Having not seen any films for weeks I'm now on my usual binge. I figure that in film the Spirit can or may break through to my spirit. Certainly She did with *Flatliners*. I'll have to think more about the Scorcese film. About the Civil War there is no doubt. The horror of that war, of all wars, but of that one in particular boggles my mind. It makes me even more resistant to the idea of yet another war, this one in the Persian Gulf. Protect us from it. And encourage the peacemakers. Let them win this one.

Also I wish to pray most fervently for Dan Herr, who I fear is not going to make it. Now that I'm back in Chicago I'll walk over to the hospital every day to see him. So much sickness, so much death, so much loss.

And I also want to pray for [my brother-in-law] Jack Durkin today who will find out whether he needs more surgery.

I saw my M.D. yesterday and he pronounces me as fit and healthy. For that, especially under the circumstances, I am very grateful indeed.

Now back to You, Spirit, which is of course You in a different manifestation. Help me to always be open to the Spirit, sensitive to Her inspirations whenever like a breeze She brushes against my face.

Sometimes You overwhelm me, especially on these early autumn days with so much beauty, so much sadness, so much color and fire, so much poignancy. I turn away from it because I do not have the time or the talent to respond. I could at times like this do nothing but write poetry all the day long.

If I go back to Grand Beach this weekend, perhaps that's what I will do, write poetry. I am surely in a mood for it.

Again I pray for all those I know who need my prayers.

PRAYER TO THE HOLY SPIRIT

Come, O Dancing God, O Spirit of Life and Love, of Beauty and Variety and Diversity, stir up my somber soul, guide me in Your light, lead me by Your fire, unleash my own leaden spirit that I may dance with You and be light for those around me and reflect Your love to all whom I love. I ask this in the name of Jesus the Lord.

Amen.

September 26, 1990 — Chicago

My Love,

I continue on my movie binge — *Cinema Paradiso* and "Civil War" yesterday, *State of Grace* today, and an opera on video tonight. Images, images, images.

The two yesterday were filled with sadness. The Civil War film is unremittingly grim — bodies, bodies, bodies. How could such things happen? Why is there so much suffering and death?

I heard two women in the elevator lobby yesterday complaining about relatives who are dying of cancer. One announced that she didn't go to Temple any more because of such things. I don't understand what good it does to blame You. The tragedy is not that a thirty-seven-year-old woman must die; the tragedy is that *anyone* must die.

It's all tragedy. I believe that You weep as we do. In this period of sickness and death all around me, the ugliness of it all overwhelms me. Yet You are aware of much worse all the time. So, all right, You have more resources to cope with tragedy. But still....

"Yet a little while," Your son Jesus says in St. John's Gospel today, "yet a little while." Life is just such a little while. One must do what one can while one can. That's what life means.

In *Cinema Paradiso* the sentimentality was so thick You could skate on it, a cry for youth and home and roots and lost love. Was the price of success too much? The filmmaker wasn't sure at the end, though his protagonist did return to his work, and with perhaps a clearer sense of his roots.

I'm lucky. My roots are where I am, more or less. I didn't have to leave all that much behind, for which many, many thanks. While I do not want to make to big a thing out of it I would surely be happy to be able to return to Christ the King parish, and that could happen if the right person is appointed pastor. So I entrust that project to Your care with the proviso as always that You know best.

PRAYER FOR UNDERSTANDING

Jesus, light of the world, help me to understand as best I can in this time of confusion and uncertainty, of mystery and bafflement, what is the purpose of my life, how I should respond to its problems, and the presence of your Father's love in all the tragedies and glories of the human condition. Grant that I may see a little more clearly.

Amen.

September 27, 1990 — Chicago

My Love,

Good news about Jack Durkin for which I am very grateful indeed. I wonder how I would survive living under such an endless threat. Dan Herr was a little better at the hospital yesterday, which is also good news, though his situation is problematic still. I'll return to Grand Beach this weekend, unless the weather turns absolutely terrible, to collect the stuff I left behind and to spend some time praying and recollecting — a kind of mini-retreat before the craziness of the next two months begins. I'll try to get in the mood for it by doing some poetry

In St. John's Gospel today, Jesus is beginning his prayer for his disciples, as beautiful a passage as human talent has ever set on paper. Clearly it is a composition written long after the event. But just as clearly it could not have been written unless there was a memory that Jesus had displayed such sentiments.

In this, as in all things, Jesus reflects Your love for us, Your tender, passionate concern for every human. You worry about us, as every mother worries about her children. And You have so much to worry about! In Gluck's opera *Alceste,* which I saw last night (dullsville to tell the truth), Apollo descends from a machine to save the day — classic *deus ex machina*. You don't play the game that way, though. I hope You won't be offended if I say that sometimes I wish You would! Your promise is that in the end You will wipe away all tears, just as a human mother wipes away all tears. I believe that, of course, and I believe that Jesus accurately reflects Your passionate concern for each of us. It would be better, I think, if, instead of trying to figure out the implications of that concern for explaining human life, I accepted it and lived in its comfort.

Help deepen my faith, especially over this weekend, which I hope to devote to prayer.

September 28, 1990 — Grand Beach

My Love,

Despite the rain I came up to Grand Beach with the intent to make a retreat. However, I had to catch up with a pile of mail. So I'll have to start tomorrow morning. I brought no books and no work so I should have a fair amount of time for praying and recollecting. What I hope to do tomorrow, with Your help, is write a poem which pulls together my recent experiences and meditate on that.

The transition to Chicago was easier than I thought, mostly because one of my sociological projects came to nothing: the data didn't fit the theory, which happens all too frequently in this problematic world.

I want to renew my prayer for Dan Herr. Give him back his health. I don't want to lose him.

September 29 — Grand Beach

SEPTEMBER SONG 1990
IN MEMORIAM DANIEL J. HERR

A dune ravaged by manic winter waves,
Undercut, obliterated, swept away.
So seems the edifice of my life:
The phone will not ring again,
The guest will not come again,
The bonds will never be restored.

I hate this month of death
Of I.C.U. monitors and strained sympathy,
Of hospital room, wake, and funeral Mass,
Of falling leaves and failing life,
Of stone-numb memory and diminished faith,
This damnable month of death.

Grief drunk, my hope staggers and stumbles
Into the cold and hostile night,
An addict to ideas, projects, dreams,
Which will pass and be forgotten with the rest.
Ecclesiastes had it all along:
Life is vanity, death snuffs it out.

Before long I will follow them,
A year or two, ten, twenty,
It makes little difference;
For they will come too soon:
My deathbed, my wake, my funeral Mass,
Then a fading memory for a very few.

My energies and expectations
Will, save in archives, disappear.
My pointless pilgrimage forever ended
My brief trip between oblivions will be done.

A chipmunk, bathed in sun, scurries by the pane,
There is still time, all the time,
Love and life are as strong as death,
And, ultimate truth, yet stronger still.

September 30 — Grand Beach

SEPTEMBER SONG 1990 II
IN MEMORIAM JOHN M. KRUMP

A wife and children, says the Trappist monk,
Innocent of how families can break the heart,
That is what I miss the most.
Kids I surely like, even teens,
And women I do certainly enjoy
Yet I do not mourn their loss.

A journey never taken
A gate never entered
A sweetness never tasted
An adventure never risked
A dream never realized —
A choice without regrets.

Other drummers were sounding a different beat
In the woods and in the hills,
Up the river and down,
Inviting my eager feet to join
A march to another destination
On a pilgrimage of grace.

Now the trip is almost over —
A jet stream ride of sound and lights,
A expedition into dark and silence,
Soaring mystery and desperate delight
Sublime excitement and abject failure;
And I am weary, worn, and tired.

I peer into the black hole of death
Where all is crushed into a single dot,
And see, what? absurdity or meaning?
Or somehow a strange blend of both?
Darkness at the end of light?
Or light at the end of darkness?

The light came into the dark
And the dark could not put it out.

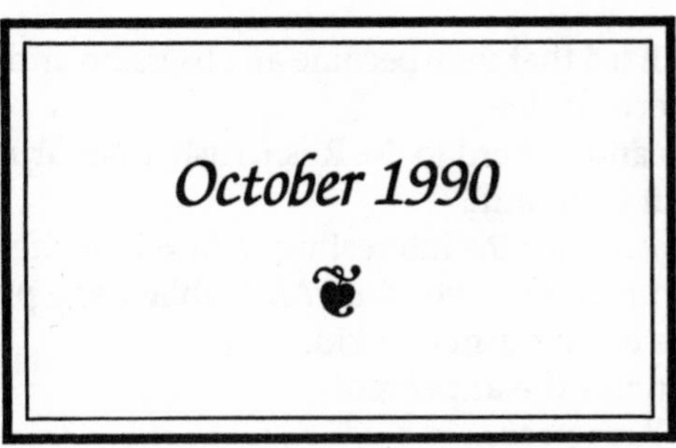

October 1, 1990 — Grand Beach

My Love,

Dan's funeral this morning. Grim experience. Several times in the day I had the instinct to call him. I suppose that will go away with time. There is a gap in my life, as I said in the poem, something that will never be filled.

Grant him rest and peace. Help those of us who miss him to remember his wit and generosity.

I'll be back tomorrow. I'm not functioning too well just yet.

October 2, 1990 — Chicago

My Love,

Better today, but still with a sense of loss and emptiness. September was a terrible month with all that death. Funny, when I was a young priest I was good at dealing with death and weak at expressing sympathy. Now I'm good at sympathy and poor at dealing with death.

As I said in the poem, I plunge on with all my plans and projects, realizing that they're not all that important, but also with nothing much else to do. Since I began this reflection, the phone has rung five or six times and the fax once. None of this matters much from the point of view of eternity, but we seem to live in time and not eternity. The trick is to work hard on the affairs of life but not so hard that they become an obsession and replace the ultimate concerns of life.

Easy to say and so hard to do. Rush, rush, rush. Truly an addict to work. Will it ever end?

Still I'm grateful for the interesting and exciting life with which You've blessed me. It's never dull! And while I age physically, so far I retain the enthusiasm of a kid.

And sometimes the anger too!

Grant me Your peace.

October 3, 1990 — Chicago

My Love,

The wicked, I learn from today's reading, prosper. They trap Jesus in the garden, they occasion laments from the psalmist. There isn't any question that wickedness runs rampant in the world and that people do wicked things and that indeed some men and women surely are wicked. Saddam Hussein, for example, has brought terrible misery to the hundreds of thousands of guest workers in the Middle East. One of the weaknesses of the modern consciousness is to psychologize away wickedness, save for a few convenient symbols of evil like Hitler and perhaps Stalin: "The kids who brutalized the Central Park jogger were victims themselves and hence not responsible for the evil they did."

Surely it is not up to us to judge the moral state or the emotional freedom of wicked men and women. It is up to You to judge them, but it is up to us to call wickedness by its proper name and to protect those we can from wickedness. We don't do a very good job.

Why You tolerate the behavior of wicked men and women is Your problem. I don't propose to try to solve it for You — not mind You, that You asked. But we must not excuse wickedness on the grounds that it is Your will or that the victimizers are socially or psychologically weakened. Perhaps they are but it does not make much difference to the victim, does it?

I don't know why I wandered off on this tangent this morning. Maybe I'm angry because of all the loss of the last month. Or maybe I had to get some of this off my chest. Anyway, protect us all against the wicked.

PRAYER FOR PROTECTION

O gracious God who has given us life and health, protect us against human wickedness, against the envious and the malicious, the ambitious and the demented, the sick and the crazy, against those who hate us and would destroy us. May we resist them with charity and patience, but protect those we love against them nonetheless. And do You, guardian of our homes and our love, keep them away from our door. We ask for this protection in the name of Jesus the Lord. Amen.

October 6, 1990 — Chicago

My Love,

I'm a week into the two-month hustle of October/November and already fed up with the rushing. I was at the Mary O'Hara concert out in Itasca last night and could hardly keep my eyes open. Why have I permitted myself to be stretched out so far?

As always I don't dislike any particular obligation; it's the cumulation of them that is too much. I don't see any way out of the commitments of the next two months. Perhaps I should not be going to Arizona. Perhaps the Bangkok conference is nutty. Yet how could I have said no to the former and ignored the opportunity of the latter?

Too much, too much, too much.

Oddly enough, now I want to be lazy. I want to read the pile of novels I have on my shelf. I want to watch the three operas I have on tape. There is no time. Perhaps next week. Perhaps then I'll begin to slow down from the running and the catching up.

I am tired and discouraged and confused despite Your wonderful Indian summer Saturday.

October 7, 1990 — Chicago

My Love,

I continue to be confused and discouraged, tired, depressed, hassled, worn, weary. I don't know what it is — all the deaths, low-level infections, rushing about. I really don't want to work, don't even want to go to the Bears game this afternoon, don't want to do anything except read novels and watch operas on video, neither one of which do I have time to do. Am I getting *that* old?

Yesterday I read a book about marriage laws in the first millennium and a half and the absurd impediments based on relationships. The author thought it was a scheme to prevent rich people from having heirs so that the Church could appropriate their property. My own guess is that it was an attempt to restrain the abuse of marriage for property purposes, though there is no opposition between the two explanations.

I shake my head in dismay, however, at the picture of the Church getting itself involved in such absurdities and being convinced that they were of divine origin, though there was nothing in the Scriptures or the early tradition to justify such rules.

I wonder if the sexual obsessions of Church leaders today will seem as absurd in years to come? Probably.

Somehow the book discouraged me greatly. I became a priest out of a desire to serve the Church. Pretty clearly the Church as an institution doesn't want my service. I now understand about the community and the tradition and believe I'm serving them as well as I can. Yet it is discouraging to realize how stupid and blind and venal Church leaders have been down through the centuries. They're humans and we cannot expect better, at least not much better. But do they have to be so dumb?

I must go to a birthday party after the football game tonight. I want only to come home and relax. I have begun to hate all social obligations. I'm even getting out of the game next week no matter what happens today.

I just want to be left alone. Help me in this time of discouragement, I beg You.

October 8, 1990 — Chicago

My Love,

I continue to be terribly depressed. The weather — drizzle, dark, and dank — doesn't help. But I was discouraged when the weather was nice.

I'm sure that the impact of all the sickness and death last month has caught up with my unconscious. I am surely in no shape to undertake a trip to Asia.

I wonder if I'm physically ill. My stomach has been uneasy for the last week and was particularly bad yesterday. Some minor infection which combines with the weather and the deaths to wipe me out. Again I beg You to help me out of this mess.

October 9, 1990 — Chicago

My Love,

Still troubled. I read the chapter on seminaries in Jason Barry's book a few minutes ago. It was hardly calculated to pick me up out of the dumps. What a terrible mess we have made out of the priesthood in the years since the Council. Horrible leadership — stupid, venal, cowardly.

I saw Mario Cuomo last night at a Democratic function. What a great man he is! He spoke to me about hope for both the Catholic Church and the Democratic Party. And he added that perhaps neither of us would live long enough to see the fruits of that hope.

I'm not so sure about the Party. If George Bush continues to foul up, it has a great future, despite itself. As for the Church, however, there are no solid human grounds for hope today at all, at all. The leadership from top to bottom with only a few exceptions is corrupt and worse, stupid. All its actions are counterproductive even on its own terms. Sometimes I think the next papal election will change matters, but in the past times the elections have only made matters worse.

The only hope is in You and Your love for us and for the Church no matter how battered it is. You and Your Holy Spirit certainly have Your work cut out for You. So like Governor Mario, I have hope, but the hope is in You. Please help me out of this depression.

October 10, 1990 — Chicago

My Love,

The rain and cold continue, four straight days.

I'm a little better today, though still discouraged. I have also discovered that somehow I have erased all the reflective entries from

April to September. No great loss, because they can't be erased from the permanent hard disk which is Your mind. However, this accident reminds me that I should read, probably when I'm in Arizona next week, last year's journal — find out who the one is who wrote it!

Thanks for the idea for the title of the new novel. *An Embarrassment of Miracles* has the right sound about it.

It's odd that I can function well on most levels of my existence despite this melancholy. Eventually I can and will snap out of it with Your help. But that can happen only when the time has come.

I'll be back tomorrow.

PRAYER IN MELANCHOLY

O gracious Lord, who created us to be happy in Your service, lift the clouds from my spirit that I may bask in the rays of Your saving sunlight. Come to my melancholy soul and set it on fire with love and joy so that I might better serve You in whatever days I have left in my life. I ask this in the name of Jesus the Lord.

Amen.

October 11, 1990 — Chicago

My Love,

The sun is out for the first time in five days, though there is fog beneath us. Thus far, at any rate, the reappearance of light has not helped me out of the dumps I've been in. The book on the police I read yesterday didn't help, that's for sure. The world is a terrible place and no one in it sees the terror more acutely than does a cop.

Compared to their work, that of a priest is easy. We see a lot of good people. I'm afraid they don't.

I've been reading St. John's account of the passion. It reveals in its own way how bad humankind can be. Yet You love us. I've had plenty of opportunity in the last few days to reflect on how bad I can be — not like those who killed Jesus or persecuted David (about whom he is complaining in the psalms all the time) — but still, given my opportunities, bad enough. Sure some of my faults were mistakes, errors in judgment, thoughtlessness, but that only mitigates my responsibility.

On some of them perhaps I can do better with Your help now that I see the situation a little more clearly. That thought does not cheer me up much. When will this depression go away?

And what is causing it?

I do love You. And know how much You love me.

PRAYER FOR FORGIVENESS

O God, You who are the personification of forgiveness, You whom Jesus depicted as the indulgent farmer, the father of the prodigal son, the Good Samaritan, forgive me all that I have done wrong in life and help me to understand that Your eagerness to forgive me is greater by far than my need to be forgiven. Grant that I may believe that in Your love, I am already forgiven. I ask this in the name of the same Jesus Your son.

Amen.

October 15, 1990 — Chicago

My Love,

I'm sorry I missed the last two days. My schedule was off and when that happens I forget prayer, which says a lot about my prayer life doesn't it?

I'm kind of dragging along. It would help if I could swim, but the building's pool isn't functioning. I walked six miles yesterday, but that didn't seem to help.

I have an idea for another novel — a charismatic, dedicated churchman who finally falls apart. This one is a tragedy, the first tragedy I've ever written. We'll have to see how it works.

I'm off again to Tucson tomorrow. The change might do me good.

I find that I'm touchy and impatient. Someone tried to exit on my floor this morning while I was entering the elevator. He blocked my way in because he thought it was floor 44. I wanted to take his head off. I didn't say anything (of course, I'm still good at impulse control), but the fury I felt astonished me.

Only a few weeks away from Grand Beach and already tied up in knots.

No, that's not it. Tucson probably won't help. It's the result, I am sure, of all the death which has happened lately. That will just have to wear itself out.

I love You. Help me out of the morass I'm in.

October 16, 1990 — Chicago

My Love,

I'm off to Tucson in a couple of hours. I'm not sure how that will change my life. Same old thing in a different locale. At least I'll be able to swim again. I bet the pool here isn't finished till I leave for Bangkok.

Dinner last night was delightful. Thank You for it.

I read in St. John this morning about the burial of Jesus, a perfect passage for my present mood. I'll be buried too someday, sooner rather than later. All my work, all my output won't matter much. I'll probably be written off as an author of steamy novels.

As You can see, I'm still in a terrible mood. I see no immediate hope of getting out of it. It's not that nothing is going right, because most things are. It's rather that nothing seems to matter anymore.

I know that I have to live with this depression until it passes. I know that I must continue my work and appear to be happy so that others will not worry about me. I know You will salvage me from it all in Your own good time.

So I keep plugging along. Help me, please.

I love You.

October 17, 1990 — Tucson

My Love,

I'm in Tucson now. Lovely weather. For some reason I've begun to feel better. Maybe it's just being away from the demands of Chicago if only for a little bit. It is more peaceful here. Or maybe the time has come to break out of my dark mood.

Anyway, as I was driving in from the airport, I thought how fortunate I am to have this other life as a professor out here where I can relax and avoid the worst of the winter and have another set of friends. I am most grateful to You for providing it to me.

Last night was [Professor] Erika's eightieth birthday party and Festschrift presentation night. It was all very moving. Her students and friends really love her, though there was an ambivalence which I think enters into the relationships of all psychologists because they have labels, relatively hostile, to slap on all human behavior.

St. John's Gospel today is about the empty tomb — a marvelous metaphor for the human condition. Jesus is gone, he is not here. But where is he? Ah, good question — not only for Jesus but for all our dead and for ourselves too. The empty tomb represents the mystery of life. Why is it here, what does it mean?

The woman sitting next to me last night told me about the death of her first husband — a Jewish agnostic. In his last moments, he sat up straight, stretched out his hands and with a vast smile on his face said, "Jesus, I'm ready! Take me with You!" Then he fell back and with the same beatific smile died.

Wow! That's pretty spectacular. Not nearly enough discussion about incidents like that, signs of the transcendent, rumors of angels.

You have Your signs everywhere, don't You!

Thank You for the partial recovery which seems to have taken place.

I know You love me.

October 18, 1990 — Tucson

My Love,

Late to prayer today because I got tied up with computer problems and novel revision. The novel revision would come now, just when I have only ten days before my departure for Bangkok. The weather here is wonderful. It would be nice to be outdoors.

Maybe it's the change to Arizona. Maybe it's the weather. Or maybe I'm just preoccupied with the novel, but my depression seems to have lifted — gone as mysteriously as it came.

The Gospel is about the women going to the tomb very early in the morning the first day of the week. Resurrection begins, the promise of the same for us also begins. At lunch today my friend Doug told a deathbed story much like the one I heard Monday night. Life is too important, as Chesterton said, to ever be anything but life. We shall all laugh again. We shall all be young again.

I seem to be experiencing a resurrection now despite the swamp of work that pulls me down — a resurrection which comes from no effort of mine. That's a perfect prediction of what it's going to be like, a sacrament. Help me never to forget that sacrament.

October 19, 1990 — Tucson

My Love,

My astonishing resurrection continues — even though I have worked intensively since coming here. Maybe it's getting away from Chicago, I don't know. And I don't have to know. All I have to do is thank You, and to understand that this rebirth of hope, what else to call it, is a sacrament, a hint of what life is all about.

I read the story today of Jesus meeting Mary Magdalene in the garden after his resurrection. What a beautiful story! In this, as in other matters, Jesus is a sacrament of You. You are as tender and as gentle as Jesus was in the garden — and also a guarantor of life and renewed life.

I hope I can finish the novel revisions before the day is over so that I have some time tomorrow to reflect at greater length on resurrection and thus deepen my faith in its reality. I'm still rushing and working at breakneck speed in the hope that soon the obligations will be swept away.

I should know better than that!

October 20, 1990 — Tucson

My Love,

Only ten days more before I leave for Thailand. It fits the adventuresome part of my psyche to make the trip.

It does not, alas, fit the resistances of my body to moving around from one place to another, much less from one part of the world to another.

Next week, with its meeting in Cincinnati and other amusements, will not be good preparation. Help me to be reasonably relaxed as I approach the trip. I am not worried about the Thailand part because I'll have a chance to rest for a week once I'm there. It's coming back into the maelstrom of my Chicago life which will be difficult.

Help me to do that too.

It will be interesting to see when I go back home tomorrow whether the feeling of rebirth that came upon me almost at once out here is duplicated in Chicago. I hope so. But even if it's not I'll have a hint of what has happened.

The Gospel today is about doubting Thomas. Boy, do I fit that category — not explicit doubt, but rather a life in which confidence and faith are bracketed issues.

I want to pray for all my friends from the old group, especially today.

October 21, 1990 — Tucson

My Love,

I'm leaving Tucson at this gracefully early morning hour, sitting in the airport, waiting to board the plane.

Again I thank You for the laptop which makes air travel less dull and more useful, though not, alas, less tiring. It looks like the Compaq will improve things even more with the desktop and the laptop becoming identical. I won't have to fret with different key locations.

Anyway I thank You for the interlude here in Tucson. It was busy and hectic but somehow relaxing. Maybe I'll come out again in early January — though I surely miss much about Chicago when I'm here. I don't miss the rush, however.

The Mass at Our Mother of Sorrows went well yesterday. It seems odd to say that the Mass is fun, except it's supposed to be a celebration and it ought to be fun, despite all the creeps who want to make it dull or stodgy or pompous.

Thomas's problem in the Gospel I've been reading is that he is a hardheaded realist about the meaning and purpose of life. Thomas is convinced that wonderful things don't happen. His world is a dull and prosaic place. He would have made a good academic or journalist.

There is a bit of Thomas in everyone, in me included, or especially. In theory I believe in wonder and surprise. Indeed I've heard several wonder stories since I've been here in Tucson. I write books about wonder and novels in which surprise happens all over the place.

Yet often in my daily life I'm the dullest and most prosaic of persons, worried about getting enough sleep, not eating too much, keeping my daily schedule, finishing my work, getting my swim in.

All of these are necessary if not essential activities, I tell myself. But the weariness which comes from such activity is not conducive to being open to wonder and surprise.

I am making excuses for which I am sorry. All I can say, I guess, is that I want to be open to the wonderful, but I need Your help to overcome ordinary human weakness and exhaustion, especially in the fast-paced life I lead.

Help me to say with Thomas, "My Lord and my God!"

I do love You.

October 22, 1990 — Chicago

My Love,

Today's Gospel is about Peter and Your son Jesus after the resurrection — "Peter, do you love me?" Jesus asked. Poor Peter sounds almost in tears.

I can hear You asking me the same question. "Andrew, do you love Me?" and myself replying, "Lady, You know that I love You!"

But how often in the course of a day does it seem that I don't love You or at least am indifferent to Your love? How often indeed do I remember in my rush through life even my human loves? I'm so busy doing so many things that love seeps out of my life like blood escaping a wound.

I am going to try as best I can at least to begin my day and end it on my knees — and also to remember You when I come or go from my apartment.

I've tried that before, but I'm going to try it again. I ask for Your help. If I can do these things they will begin, I think, to reshape my life and make me a better person and a better lover.

Please help me. This time I intend to stick to it.

And thank You for my resurrection from the gloom!

October 23, 1990 — Chicago

My Love,

I am really trying to remember the "presence of God" resolution I made yesterday. I've not had too much success, but have done a little better. I intend to continue to work on it with all the vigor I have. I know full well that I cannot do it without Your help — not anything, but especially something that I have failed on so often since I was in the seminary. And I fail for the same reason, the busy demands of my busy, busy life (self-induced).

If I can improve a little in this respect, my life will be very different indeed. Please help me.

I'm turning to Acts in my morning readings. When I was a boy and read this book of the Scripture for the first time, I found it exciting. Now, even though I know its literary form and realize it's not quite history the way I understand history, some of the wonder has, alas, worn off. Also it is now a familiar story. I hope that as I read it this time around, the wonder returns.

For the whole history of Christianity's spread is a story of wonder, of astonishing surprises. I often think that the most astonishing is that the firm has survived all the idiocy of its leaders. And the corruption and the sinfulness.

I hope to make that the theme of my next novel.

And I hope that this reading of the Acts will renew and deepen my hope.

I love You. Help me to keep You in mind during the day.

October 24, 1990 — Chicago

My Love,

I'm at O'Hare Airport this morning on the way for three talks in Cincinnati. At this hour it is easy to be tired and discouraged and to wonder what the point of it all is. As You know, I'm going because the money earned will be used to help people. I wouldn't need so much money if I didn't have such a large support staff. And I have the support staff because I write novels which make the money. It's all so crazy. This morning I think about retiring, not because I've run out of ideas but because it would be the best way to escape from all the burdens imposed upon me — or that I impose upon myself.

I am grateful to You for all the help You gave me yesterday to remember Your presence. It was much better than I thought it would be and I was conscious in a funny sort of way that I was being reminded. Help me to continue to think of You and Your presence during this trip today.

I need Your help and Your friendship in the years ahead as old age and infirmity creep up on me. So far I show no signs of either. I am grateful for my good health, but I realize that I have made far more of these trips to airports than lie ahead of me. Dying, I must remember, is no big thing, just part of life.

Again I ask You to guard and protect me on my trip to Thailand, next week. It's a crazy scheme but as You well know I can't resist adventure, no matter how crazy it is. At least it will be adventure in comfort.

October 25, 1990 — Cincinnati

My Love,

I continue to remember Your presence during the day, for which many thanks. Help me to keep it up. Please.

October 26, 1990 — Chicago

My Love,

Now comes the final rush before I leave for Thailand. A lot of things to worry about while I'm gone. My office at the National Opinion Research Center with Mary in the hospital. Jack Durkin's operation. The book contract negotiation. The Chicago election. I can never remember leaving the country with more problems on my mind. Moreover, when I come back the problems will still be there and I'll be a shambles in having to deal with them. It is not only possible that things will go wrong, they will certainly go wrong. Given half a chance, people foul things up.

I suppose I should conclude that I ought not to leave. Of course I will leave, and to hell with all the things that can go wrong. I leave them in Your hands and trust You to take care of me and my interests while I'm gone.

This may or may not be a great adventure, but at least there'll be a few days of rest in Thailand, which will be nice.

I saw the movie *Mr. Destiny* last night and was quite impressed by Michael Caine playing Yourself. The point about You in the film is that You loved the Jim Belushi character, no matter how much of a nerd he was. Your final words, on the lips of Mr. Caine of course, are the only answer to human *angst* and to my own personal angst about what is ahead of me: *"Trust me!"*

Okay, fair enough, I will trust You, as best I can and with Your help.

October 27, 1990 — Chicago

A lovely, lazy Saturday morning, my Love, though as is typical in my life not lazy enough. I have a visit to make, a Mass to celebrate, and a dinner to eat. And a Notre Dame game to watch, and data to prepare, and an article to write. How awful! How do I get into these binds? Too active an imagination, I guess. Ideas explode in my head like firecrackers.

I read in my spiritual reading yesterday a nice little essay called "Someone Keeps Sending Me Flowers," the someone, of course, being You — You who also send crisp autumn days and fun parties and good friends and love. I don't appreciate any of these enough. Nor do I appreciate the grace You've sent me the last couple of days to keep me on the track of remembering You.

But I am grateful for Your flowers and for everything else.

I love You. Help me to keep loving You. And to continue to be open to all the gifts You send me.

October 28, 1990 — Chicago

My Love,

It's the last Sunday in October and hence return to standard time. The sun comes up earlier (thank You) and we get an extra hour sleep (I didn't), but darkness comes so early in the afternoon. This Sunday reminds us that we're losing a little bit more light every day and will till Christmastime. For a light-sensitive creature like myself that's bad news.

Incidentally, how did I ever survive in that basement rectory room for three years with hardly any light at all! I'm not complaining. Many had to suffer worse, as You surely know. I'm just astonished that I put up with it as long as I did.

Somehow I'm still not excited about the trip to Asia. In principle it's exciting, but I dread the terrible physical impact and especially the crunch when I come back. Take care of me on the trip and please don't let me get sick as I so often do when I travel.

When I retire I will solemnly promise never to travel again!

The retirement impulse grows stronger, not to actually stop work but to shed much of the junk which has loaded up my life.

The reading today is about the coming of the Spirit at Pentecost. The psalm celebrates Your protection. And my spiritual reading does too. But I guess I'm just not all that enthused on this late October Sunday morning. I'm not depressed like I was before I went to Arizona. But I am discouraged over all the work I've done and the little impact that it's had.

That's not true, is it? The novels have had an impact, but they have also been so terribly distorted. So many people write me that they understand You better because of them, and that's why I can't stop doing them. So why do I get so discouraged?

I know the answer to these reflections before I write them down. I must trust You as Michael Caine demanded in Your name in the film the other day. I know that You love me and will take care of me and use my work for what *You* want. I consign myself totally to You and Your love.

I'm sure that before the day is over I will come alive and be hopeful again.

It will surely be nice to be able to swim again starting tomorrow.

A PRAYER ON THE LAST SUNDAY IN OCTOBER

O God, who brings us both light and darkness, I mourn the loss of light and accept the coming of darkness. Grant that as darkness grows stronger and light weaker in the days and weeks to come, my faith in Your triumph over sin and death may be as certain as the eventual return of light. I ask this in the name of Jesus, the light of the world.

Amen.

October 29, 1990 — Chicago

My Love,

If I were superstitious Irish, I'd say You were getting even with me for my reluctance to fly off to Southeast Asia tomorrow. I have a fever this morning and that puts everything in jeopardy. Maybe it will be gone by this afternoon and I'll be able to leave in the morning and maybe not. We'll have to see what happens and what the doctor says.

I know enough after all these years of life to realize that there is no point in fighting what You permit to happen. If I am not to go — and now I find that I *want* to — then so be it.

Usually I get sick while I'm traveling. This is the first time I've been sick *before* the traveling begins. Maybe I ought not to travel at all. How many times have You heard me say that!

Anyway we will see what happens. To tell the truth, I feel sick and like I'm getting sicker. Excuse me.

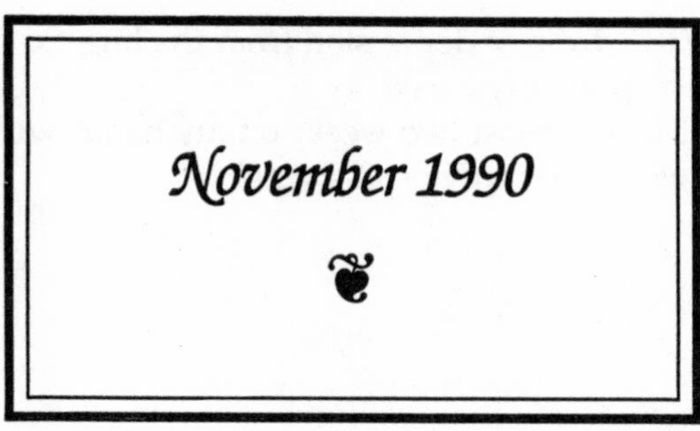

November 1990

November 2, 1990 — Chicago

My Love,

Well, when You want to send a message, You don't fool around, do You?

I was not to go to Bangkok and You made that clear by letting me get pneumonia! I am so grateful that the plane was delayed long enough in L.A. for me to be able to get off it and come home. I am also grateful that Dr. Marty Phee began treatment before I left with the antibiotics that they use for pneumonia these days. Hence I am already recovering — no fever today. However, the trip is off. I've notified the UNDA people. I expect I won't be forgiven — people too seldom forgive those who let them down. No matter how valid the excuse is, they don't believe it.

Pneumonia is a pretty good excuse.

Jack Durkin is in surgery now. They're removing the parotic gland and the lymph nodes around it, all of the latter of which are clean. Sounds like a repeat of the surgery six years ago. Astonishing! It will be devastating for them — four surgeries in nine years. Please help them!

The autumn continues to sadden with sickness and death. I don't mean my sickness either because I was ill really only for two days.

I was attacked by a priest in the *Chicago Sun Times* today. Usual clerical culture garbage. I must be improving. I didn't even think of responding!

Marty warned me of depression from the bug. So far I don't feel that way. Only very weak.

So now I have almost two weeks on my hands without anything scheduled — except hospital visits.

November 3, 1990 — Chicago

My Love,

No fever now for twenty-four hours and not much coughing. But I'm still weak and very depressed. Also I had a terrible night last night — the worst kind of dreams in which I am again called upon to do the impossible — dreams I couldn't end by waking up. Illness and medication, I'm sure. It's not fun to be ill.

Thank You for the health with which You've blessed me through the years. Take care of me in the years to come. I offer up to You my sufferings from weariness and depression and my sense that everything is worthless — which of course I know it isn't.

November 5, 1990 — Chicago

My Love,

Being sick isn't easy. I prayed a little bit but not much. My awareness of Your presence, which had improved greatly the week before, vanished. Now I must recapture it again, perhaps by praying on my knees before I leave the apartment. But the point here is that sickness, like everything else, diminishes prayer unless it is a habit as deeply ingrained as eating and drinking and sleeping.

If my life ends in sickness, as is most probable, I will pray in that final sickness only to the extent that I have developed habits of prayer before. All the more reason to work on prayer now.

Without Your help I cannot pray. You gave me lots of help before. Give it to me again.

I suffer from some residual disappointment because of the loss of the Bangkok trip, though I don't miss recovering from jet lag. I offer up to You for peace in the world the preparatory work I put into the trip and the disappointment because it did not occur.

And I thank You for the lack of jet lag!

November 7, 1990 — Chicago

My Love,

Still under the weather. I went out for lunch and for Dick Phelan's political victory party last night and felt pretty good till the end of the latter. But it was too busy a day. So I'm exhausted this morning. It's going to be a long, slow road back, and Dr. Phee tells me I'm going to have to get used to being tired and depressed — utterly devoid of energy.

I expended a lot of it yesterday in one big whosh! and am paying the price today.

Help me to accept patiently the biological necessity of getting over my illness.

I'm just so tired.

I love You.

November 9, 1990 — Chicago

My Love,

Still sick, almost two weeks now. Worse, I had a relapse yesterday with a return of fever. I accept this illness and the weariness that goes with it as part of my life and do not complain about it. But I do pray that You help me to get better and then to get stronger.

I love You.

November 10, 1990 — Chicago

My Love,

At last I am beginning to recover. Thank You very much! I haven't been so sick since the surgery on my thyroid. This illness has been a good lesson for my humility. One can't control one's life. All my splendid plans for Bangkok were wiped out by an insignificant little bug. Indeed all my plans for the time between now and Christmas were put into jeopardy (and still are because one good morning does not total recovery make).

I'll continue to be influenced by the effects of those tiny bacteria for weeks to come. I'll be tired and discouraged — even more than usual. I must, on the one hand, accept the inevitability of this weakness and, on the other hand, try to take it into account as the time before Christmas draws near.

Thank You again for the apparent beginning of true recovery. Help me not to overdo it. And grant that the recovery be complete and that there may be no more relapses.

PRAYER AT THE END OF AN ILLNESS

O Lady Love, thank You for beginning the restoration of my health. Grant that I may learn from this sickness the fragility of my human organism and my total dependence on You. May my recovery be complete so that I may serve You with renewed enthusiasm. Finally, I pray that I may learn from my illness how hard it is to pray when I am sick and that therefore I may work ever more diligently on my habits of prayer.

I ask this of Jesus Your son who came at Christmastime to heal the whole world.

Amen.

November 11, 1990 — Chicago

My Love,

I've been sick now for over two weeks, much of the month of November shot, no major work really done, no tasks accomplished.

Silly line isn't it? Does it suggest that there may be a strain of a workaholic in me after all?

Actually I don't feel that way most of the time. I accept the delay as necessary and put off the next novel and statistical analysis of elections until December. But what will I feel like in December? How long will this sickness continue? What about my Christmas shopping, which ought to start at the end of this week? And my trip to New Orleans for the American Academy of Religion at the end of the week? Surely I will be able to make that, won't I?

Kind of random wandering, isn't it? I'm sorry. I do love You. Help me to get better as soon as possible.

PRAYER FOR PATIENCE

Gracious Lord, You who created everything in a Big Bang and yet let the process go on for billions of years, teach me to practice the balance between patience and enthusiasm. Grant that I may never become lethargic and that I also may not too often be impulsive and compulsive in my own work. Help me to understand the rhythms of the days and the seasons of my own life and to make those rhythms the paradigms for my work. I ask this in the name of Jesus Our Patient Lord.

Amen.

November 12, 1990 — Chicago

I'm now well on the mend, barring another relapse. Thank You once again. It's been an unusual experience. I've had a chance to watch a lot of TV!

I'm on my way out to see [Dr.] Marty Phee this morning to get an okay to resume life. He called last night to tell me that his wife is dying and would I please say the funeral Mass, very apologetic about putting pressure on me — after treating me for almost twenty years! And of course he's keeping his appointments this morning even though dear Kate is dying.

So much death this autumn, so much death. The movie was right, we must learn to let go.

Help me to react to Marty this morning the way You want me to.

And grant that I am truly over this awful pneumonia!

I love You.

November 13, 1990 — Chicago

My Love,

Sometimes these past two weeks I wonder why I write all the details of my illness to You. You know them already, being in some sense at least the tolerator of the illness, and after all, don't I have more important things to talk to You about?

However, those who love me want to hear from me about how I feel, and *You* love me. Therefore it follows with neat scholastic logic that You also want to hear how I feel. So I guess You have to put up with all the nagging details.

The doctor said I was recovering yesterday but not recovered. I feel a little better each morning but my energy flags toward the end of the day and my fever goes up.

Pneumonia is not something to fool with obviously. Two weeks and I *still* feel exhausted, even at 9:15 in the morning!

Dr. Phee and his family are doing well with his wife's terminal illness. So is she. They all wish it would be over, too. Please help them.

Faith under such circumstances continues to impress me. Human hope is enormous and resilient and finally, I think, not to be overcome by all the agnosticism in the world. If one looks not for proofs but for signs, hope is a powerful sign indeed. And a religion like ours, which underpins hope with marvelous metaphors and stories, can't be beaten despite all the folly of our leaders.

The readings today both in the Psalms and in Acts were about Your power. I see that power manifested in the resiliency of the human body in the face of illness, which I am now experiencing, and in the resiliency of human hope, Kate Phee's, even when the body finally fails.

Strengthen my faith in Your power and my hope in Your goodness.

PRAYER FOR PROTECTION

O great angels of heaven, so often ignored now by us if remembered and honored by others, messengers of God and protectors of humans, stretch forth your power and might, protect us from war and sickness and injustice and accident and, as I used to pray, may one of you always be at my side to light, to guard, to rule, to guide.

Amen.

November 14, 1990 — Chicago

My Love,

I am becoming impatient, foolishly perhaps, with the pace of my convalescence. Yesterday was the day I would have returned from Thailand. Now my sickness is on *my* time and not on the meeting's time, an odd way to look at it, I suppose, but then I am odd about time.

I managed to write my long-planned article about computers yesterday but it exhausted me. It's probably not all that well done either. I feel this morning a little better than yesterday, but not much. Nor is there any appreciable decline in the fever. I ask myself, again foolishly, whether I'll ever cross the 75 percent line in my recovery.

I'm not complaining — well, not exactly. I am rather trying to explain to You as a lover how I feel. I know I can't fight the natural course of the illness and that it must run its course.

I so very much would like to swim! The lack of exercise is taking a terrible toll on my morale and on my sleep.

Sorry that I am moaning so much today. As I have said before, I accept this illness as part of my human condition. Yet I do want to get better.

I also want to pray during this illness so as to prepare for other and far worse illnesses which may lie ahead of me.

PRAYER FOR COMPLETE RECOVERY

O Loving Jesus, who came to heal those who were sick both spiritually and physically, please restore my health to its fullness, exorcise the remaining germs, help my body to regain its resistance and strength, do all these things please so that I might better serve You. Amen.

November 15, 1990 — Chicago

My Love,

With a weary body, but a cheerful heart, I began my Christmas shopping yesterday with two huge and basic purchases — books and perfume. So now I can confidently face the next six weeks with the conviction that I'm ahead of the game. I'll put up the Christmas tree tomorrow or Saturday, again getting in my preparations long before the time. But Christmas is such a wonderful time of the year that one must begin celebrating as early as possible and continue to celebrate it as long as possible.

We Catholics are very lucky to have Christmas. Of course we did invent it, didn't we? Anyway, thank *You* for Christmas! Help me this year to be more part of the festivity than ever before.

I'm off to say the memorial Mass for our classmates today. A third of them are dead already, a sobering thought if there ever was one.

I'm getting better at remembering You at least sometimes during the day. Help me to improve on that too.

PRAYER BEFORE ADVENT

Mary, my Lady, who brought new hope into the world with the coming of Your son, Jesus, stir up my hope in anticipation of Advent and Christmas. In these dark days of the year may my heart beat more rapidly with faith and joy and love as I expect the coming of the Lord. Finally help me to play a role like Yours in making straight the path of the Lord for those around me. I ask this in the name of Jesus Your son.

Amen.

November 16, 1990 — Chicago

My Love,

Are You tired of hearing me say I'm still dragging? I have so little vitality, such small amounts of energy. It's going to be this way for awhile and I accept that, but it is rough. I think I should head for Arizona right after New Year's and relax in the sun. There's no way I can go before then. All I have to do the second semester is another novel, and perhaps I'll get some of that done in Grand Beach in December if I can work up the energy.

Help me, please, to recover completely. And protect me from more sickness for my talk in New Orleans.

PRAYER FOR DEPARTED FRIENDS

O God of mercy and peace, I miss my friends who are no longer with us. Grant them light and rest in the home toward which we all journey. Give me the courage and faith to follow them on the road of this life and the bravery I will need when I cross the boundary and join them on the way home. I ask this in the name of Jesus my Lord.

Amen.

November 17, 1990 — Chicago

My Love,

I'm at Midway Airport now, leaving for the New Orleans conference in a half-hour. Still tired. But yesterday was the second day in a row without a fever, so I'm clearly on the mend. But I'm angry and irritable, which is what the doctor said would happen. So far I haven't gone after anyone, but the impulse to do so is great (actually I did lose my temper at Marshall Field's while doing some Christmas shopping but I had forgot about it). Feeling irritable after the sickness is to be expected. Taking that irritability out on others is unacceptable. I ask for Your help and assistance.

The psalm today compares You with the scorching desert wind. Apparently YOU can lose Your temper, but I can't!

Also my spiritual reading had the excellent thought that prayer is asking You to come and live with me. How marvelous! That's what I've been trying to do, but sometimes I wonder whether You enjoy listening to me. If You're a Lover, You do, and I guess that's all that matters.

I began to arrange the stars and ornaments and brightly colored lights for the Christmas tree today — not to turn them on yet but to have them ready so that I can flick a switch when I come home from Thanksgiving at Grand Beach and feel the wonder.

November 18, 1990 — New Orleans

My Love,

I'm on my way back to Chicago this Sunday afternoon after my presentation at the American Academy of Religion. It was a successful event, though being on the platform with David Tracy is an experience and a half. He is so bright and so comprehensive in his knowledge. I'm good at what I do, sometimes very good, and can be charming and witty and funny on the platform — Your all-purpose stage Irishman with a Ph.D. But David is just plain genius! Anyway, the chemistry was perfect and the session was very well received, much better than I had any reason to anticipate. The audience was positively friendly; many of them even use my novels in their classes. It was an encouraging and reassuring experience despite my weariness and exhaustion and irritability. I am very weak right now and will be exhausted when I get home, to say nothing of tomorrow, but I have definitely turned the corner and am on the mend.

So thank You for the good experience and the gracious invitation to return. And thank You too for my recovering health. Help me in the difficult week ahead — all the Thanksgiving festivities — to be as responsive and as nonirritable as possible.

November 19, 1990 — Chicago

The themes of my reading this morning are power and love: God's power as revealed in the psalm and in the speech of Stephen; God's love in the uniqueness of each of us. Your power and love, be it noted, did not save Stephen and it does not save any of us from death. But that was not part of the deal. The promise was a love which would survive death, a power which would overcome it. I believe in both Your love and Your power, though I do not pretend to understand the workings of either. Help me to live a life of faith and trust in which I respond to You like the kid should have responded to Michael Caine in the film when Caine said, "Trust me!"

I love You. Help me to understand my own uniqueness.

PRAYER FOR UNDERSTANDING

O God, who make me absolutely unique, help me to value more the person You made me to be. Protect me from comparisons and envy and discouragement over what I am not. Inspire me to become more the person that I am and that I should be. Grant that I may understand that You love me, faults and all, and that I may accept myself even as You accept me. I ask this in the name of Jesus the Lord.

Amen.

November 20, 1990 — Chicago

My Love,

Mornings are fine. Afternoons I tire. Evenings I collapse.

It will be a busy day today. Protect and guard me through it.

I love You.

November 21, 1990 — Chicago

My Love,

You know well what's tearing at my mind this afternoon.

The pneumonia is clearing out of my lungs, but there is a lump in the left lung which is either "hard pneumonia" or something much worse. They'll take another X-ray in two weeks to see if it is diminished.

I may very well be dying. Probably not, but still I may be. It could be that I have only three months to live.

I am dismayed at the thought of the tests, the CAT scans, the bronchoscopes, the surgery, the radiation, the whole business of dying with lung cancer. I do not find myself dismayed at the thought of death. Not yet, anyway. You have to die sometime and there are no good or easy ways of dying. I accept whatever You want of me. I also accept the uncertainty of the next two weeks.

If I had to guess, I'd say Marty Phee thinks it's pneumonia and the radiologist thinks it may be something worse.

Marty's case is as follows:

1. I look and feel better. Lung cancer people do not.
2. There is wheezing in the area of the lung where the concentration is.
3. Tumors don't grow to that size in two weeks (but the radiologist thinks the pneumonia might have masked it).
4. The coincidence is unlikely. Fifteen percent of pneumonia victims have X-rays which cause concern, but the concern usually vanishes with the next X-ray.
5. The mass is not where lung tumors usually appear.

So that's the case against worry and it's a strong one. That's why I say probably there's nothing wrong.

Yet I will necessarily live with uncertainty for the next two weeks and I will worry because it is in the nature of human nature to worry when mortality is involved. Do I sound like Woody Allen in *Hannah and Her Sisters?*

There is a certain poignancy to all this happening at Thanksgiving and at a time when we're celebrating the twenty-fifth anniversary of Grand Beach, a sign of the passing of time if one were needed.

I'll be as cheerful as I can, though I think the residual weakness from pneumonia, more than fear of death, in the next couple of months will inhibit me somewhat.

I will tell no one save for the Rosners so that [Dr.] Marvin can consult and let me know what his colleagues say.

I commit myself totally to Your care. Your will be done.

November 22, 1990 — Chicago

My Love,

If I do have a fatal tumor in my left lung and if I have only three months to live, I can honestly say that I am grateful for an exciting life and for all the successes. There've been failures too but success and failure are part of human life.

If there is nothing more after death, then so be it. I can nonetheless be grateful for what has happened and accept oblivion as the final part of the human condition, no matter how much it goes against such powerful human aspirations.

If, as I believe to be the case, life is too important ever to be anything but life, than I shall meet You my love for the first time and rejoice in that union which can appropriately be described by the nuptial metaphor, like a wedding night only more so.

Marty's instincts are that it is only pneumonia and so are mine, but I don't want to engage in denial. If death is in store for me in the short run, I want to be ready for it and for the suffering which will surely precede it.

Help me to have faith and courage no matter what happens.

November 23, 1990 — Grand Beach

My Love,

I seem to feel much better this morning, I mean physically better as if the pneumonia is at last losing its grip, for which many thanks.

As for the other problem, I guess I would not be feeling better if it were something more than pneumonia, which is another good sign. While it is a matter to be taken seriously and certainly not something to be denied, I have a hard time, given all the circumstances, in believing that it is any more than the end of the pneumonia. At any rate I will surely hold that it is probably just pneumonia until the contrary is proved.

But what if the contrary is proved? Well, Thy will be done.

What more can be said?

November 24, 1990 — Grand Beach

My Love,

I now seem to be recovering from the pneumonia, not completely better yet, but the pace of improvement continues to accelerate. This should be a good sign about the other problem, but I am wary of my wish being the father of the thought. Again I commit myself to Your care and Your love. Your will be done.

Yesterday's celebration of the twenty-fifth anniversary of owning this house was wonderful. It brought back many memories — happy and sad — and persuaded me that I have had a rich and full life for which I am grateful to You. Should that life end soon I have no grounds at all for complaint.

And take care of me too, please. I love You.

November 25, 1990 — Chicago

My Love,

I am now recovering rapidly, for which I am grateful to You! I swam a quarter-hour yesterday with no ill effects and I'll do a half-hour today. It's been a solid four weeks since the pneumonia bug bit me and at last I'm shaking it.

And with health comes a sudden surge of passion. I've just come up from the pool where there was no room to swim because of women swimmers and I was overwhelmed by desire for them. Of different ages and conditions, they were all suddenly vulnerable and desirable, disconcertingly, devastatingly so.

Obviously I had no intention of doing any harm to them, though a part of my personality finds the possibility of making love with them perfectly delightful.

Such desires are part of the human condition and, if not treasured or acted on, nothing more than a reminder — poignant, delicious, dangerous, humiliating — of the nature of the human condition.

Well, that must be recorded with the note that my hormones are at least working again. Not, as far as that goes, that they ever stopped.

If, as Dr. Phee said, my feelings of health are indicators of whether there is a serious problem in my lung, then there isn't one. Nonetheless it is a worry, a worry I must live with, a worry I must offer up to You, a worry that I must take seriously up to a point in case there really is a problem.

But in my new-found vigor I kind of doubt it.

My depression and weariness are gone too, for which also much thanks. And I'm at work on a new novel — just in case my life will be shorter than it might be.

I'm off to Dayton for a hard day tomorrow. It should be an acid test for my recovery.

Please take care of me and grant me life.

I love You.

November 30, 1990 — Grand Beach

My Love,

I continue to improve, but I still cough and still grow tired. It's been a whole month now, soon to be five weeks. November has been a washout. I have the feeling that I'm spinning my wheels, running around like I always do but without the energy — or the time — to do anything else.

I suppose that outburst of dissatisfaction demonstrates how much the pneumonia still affects me.

I desperately need to get control of my life again, but that is never easy and becomes impossible when sick. This whole autumn has been a time of irresistible demands, plus sickness and death.

I know I sound discouraged and frustrated. In fact, I'm probably not as bad as I sound, and I do improve each day, and I do accept the burden of sickness.

Nonetheless, I beg of You, help me to be well.

I love You.

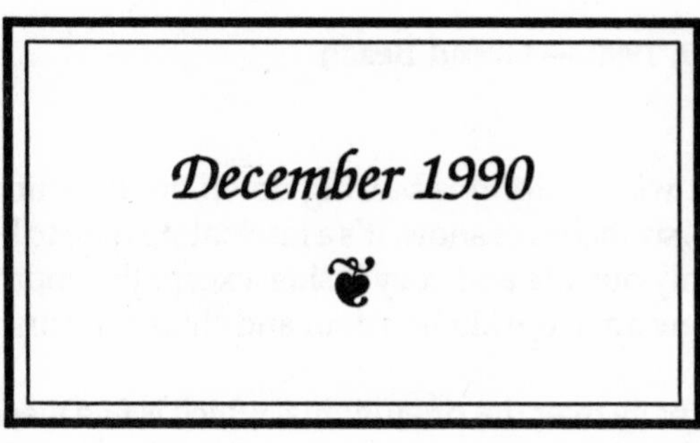

December 1990

December 2, 1990 — Grand Beach

My Love,

The lung problem is still on my mind, not interfering with anything but lurking there like a stranger hiding behind a curtain in a suspense film. It will be nice to have the matter settled on next Wednesday.

Still, I'm grateful that the pneumonia is running its course. I thank You, and for the good health I've had most of my life.

And next week I'll learn about what will happen regarding my professorship at the University of Chicago and perhaps about my possible return to Christ the King parish. In all of these matters I leave the solution to Your loving care for my own fragility and vulnerability. Please take good care of me. Obviously I want to live. Less important I would like finally to emerge victorious at the university and to return to the parish.

But Thy will be done, as Your son Jesus said, in major and minor matters.

I visited the arboretum at Lincoln Park last week for the first time and admired the wonder and glory of Your mums. It reminded me of the Aussi book *Someone Keeps Sending Me Flowers.* Flowers are a nice indicator. Even if we understand their origins and purposes in the biological kingdom completely, we still miss the point if we are not awed by their beauty and do not see in them a sign of Your love and Your beauty. Help me to enjoy them more and to be more aware of Your presence in the world.

I love You.

December 3, 1990 — Grand Beach

My Love,

The first winter storm is bearing down on us — fifty-mile-an-hour winds, six inches of snow. It's a fascinating time to be at Grand Beach, stormy outside and cozy inside, except this morning when the wind blew open the kitchen door and chilled the first floor with its breath.

I am virtually over the pneumonia, which is five weeks today, a week ahead of the doctor's prediction. Once I get this X-ray business out of the way (he said, whistling in the dark!), I'll consider myself cured.

The Gospel yesterday warned us to watch and pray because we do not know the time or the hour. We all must die. It is unlikely that I will die now, but I still might. I could, for example, get a clean bill of health from the doctor and be killed on the highway a few minutes later. Aaron Copland, the great composer, died last night (of pneumonia!) at the age of ninety. I doubt that he wanted to die either. He clung to life as I do. At the end he had to let go as I will have to let go sometime. There is no escaping death. The issue is not letting it interfere with life so that it may crown life.

Help me to live that way and when the time comes to die that way.

December 4, 1990 — Grand Beach

My Love,

Another windy, snowy day — a powerful and enthralling sight to behold. This interlude has relaxed and invigorated me. I feel ever so much better, virtually cured. Tomorrow comes the X-ray, which I have anxiously awaited for the last two weeks. I still feel confident that the problem is the pneumonia, the overwhelming odds point in that direction. Yet... here I go again.

I can rationalize and say that I have to die sometime and that it will never be easy. I can say that I accept Your will. I can say that I do not cling to life. I can say that there is no spouse or children from whom to be separated (there is no one deader than a dead priest). Yet, human that I am, I do not want to die. I do not want to suffer the prolonged death of lung cancer. I do not want to give up the things that I enjoy and, more important, the people I love.

The chances that something serious is wrong are tiny. Tomorrow I'll probably feel like an idiot. Yet for now I'll admit it, I'm scared. Not paralyzed, mind You, but concerned.

So help me through the next twenty-six hours or so. Help me to understand that no matter what happens, You love me.

As I try, however imperfectly, to love You.

December 6, 1990 — Chicago

My Love,

Thank You again — and again — for the positive verdict from the doctor yesterday! I feel so like the other nine lepers. I did thank You in my mind and heart all day but in the present state of our love affair, it really has to be done on these pages to count fully — by my rules, of course, not Yours!

Anyway the knot of infection is fraying around the edges according to the doctor, so it is pretty clearly from pneumonia and will clear away soon. Another X-ray in two weeks, but I'm basically all right, as my organism knew full well yesterday morning!

So thank You for taking such good care of me and please continue to take such good care of me, while all the time I try to place my trust in You.

I love You.

December 8, 1990 — Chicago

I'm sorry I missed yesterday. Overwhelmed by work and by the revision of the novel and the lingering effects of the pneumonia, as the doctor warned me. The sixth week is coming to an end next week and that is the time he indicated it would take. What a siege it has been!

I should not try to rush my recovery. And I should permit myself time to sleep in the afternoon like I did yesterday. There is a part of me — one that You know all too well — that wants to have a record that is not affected by being sick. It says that if I am not immune to sickness, then at least I'm immune to its effects on my work. So what if I'm behind?

I must be much easier on myself. And I must understand that the depression which continues to assail me is the result of sickness. Finally, I must resolve that there will be no work those first three weeks in Arizona.

I do love You, You know that I do. Help me to do it better. And to think of You more often each day.

December 9, 1990 — Grand Beach

I'm learning two things in this long, slow convalescence, my Love. The first is that I need more sleep than I otherwise would. The second is that I must be wary of my crabby disposition, especially at the end of the day or when under pressure.

That's easy to write, especially on this sunny morning when I feel euphoric again. But I'm not going to find it easy to live that way. I ask for Your help in the name of our love.

December 11, 1990 — Chicago

My Love,

Yet another glorious early spring day in the middle of December, for which many, many thanks. At the risk of seeming ungrateful, I'd rather be in Arizona where maybe my strength would come back more quickly, if only because there wouldn't be so many things to keep me running every day. However, I do feel better this morning, probably because I had a good night's sleep.

I'm sure *You're* tired — or You would be if You grew tired! — of my complaints about my health and physical strength and the loss of time during the past six weeks. You're probably also tired of my saying that I accept my illness and then complaining about it!

So, what can I tell You? I guess I am happy about antibiotics and that I didn't have some worse kind of illness, plus happy that I still have basically good health, happy that I am blessed with a place like Arizona to which to go, happy that the meanness of winter hasn't really come yet, happy that I'm in some control of my crankiness.

Today comes the resolution of the University of Chicago situation. If it's all the same to You, I'd like to win this one — which is not to imply that I haven't won a lot in my life as it is.

December 12, 1990 — Chicago

My Love,

I'll admit that I'm discouraged today. I do not have my strength back yet. I had to sleep this afternoon because I was so tired. Six weeks and I'm still weak. The weariness depresses me and then the depression keeps me awake at night, and that makes me weary the next morning.

The University of Chicago thing has fallen apart, as I thought it would — not definitely because nothing is ever definite there, but probably. So I lose on Christ the King and on University of Chicago. I suppose they were both long shots, romantic pipe dreams. Perhaps it would not have been good for me to win on either, much less on both. Perhaps I should know by now that I'm destined forever to be an outsider and that's my strength and my vocation. I accept that along with whatever else You plan for my life. How can I look back on the trajectories and do anything else but admire Your loving care, dare I say special loving care for me?

I just learned that my friend Jim is sick. Please take care of him and help him — and also help him to find You, or rather, as I firmly believe is the case, to realize that he has never lost You.

But, back to being an outsider. Yesterday, even though I had the loss at University of Chicago, I did have an article on Christmas and Hanukkah in the *New York Times* and was invited to dinner at the mayor's house before Christmas. Neither sounds like an outsider, does it? What a strange life!

I must learn to give up control, to cast myself into Your arms and take what comes, without worry about vindication or triumph.

I have failed often and won often, more than enough wins for one lifetime. Help me to realize that there is no point in counting things up but that rather my goal should be always to grant ever more trust to You.

December 13, 1990 — Chicago

My Love,

I am deeply concerned about Jim's health. He was on my mind for most of the night. Please grant that he may be all right.

I'm lighting the Hanukkah candle every night and listening to Christmas carols on my CD and am going to sort out presents today. I'm trying to capture the Christmas spirit. If I can continue to get the sleep, Christmas will be fun!

I'm getting lots of good reaction to the book that Dan Herr insisted on putting together from last year's reflections. I didn't intend it to be for anyone but You, but it's nice that other people find it helpful too.

Thank You for all the love and excitement in my life. You have been very good indeed to me.

December 15, 1990 — Chicago

My Love,

What a creature of weather I am! The sunlight is gone and clouds and rain obscure the city from my observation post here on the forty-seventh floor. All I have to do is to wake up and observe these conditions and a certain discouragement takes over in my soul, now made worse by the remnants of my illness. There's nothing that can be done about this reaction; it's part of the permeable boundaries which define my personality and explain my ability to tell stories. I must resist temptations to let this grimness of spirit take possession of my soul and push me into reactions which will be false to faith and charity. But I can't simply repress it either. I must acknowledge it and accept it as part of the price I pay for what I am — and also take it into account, so that it will not taint my day and my life.

I must also find time today and in days to come for more meditation and reflection on the joys of this blessed season which are invading my life through every one of my five senses: the smell of Christmas plants, the sound of Christmas music, the color of Christmas lights, the feel of Christmas wrapping paper, the taste of Christmas eggnog.

That must be my goal this weekend — let my senses be filled with Your Christmas gifts!

December 16, 1990 — Chicago

My Love,

I had dinner last night with the old St. Angela crowd, an exceedingly pleasant evening as well as an excellent dinner. They had all read my reflections from last year. Their reaction was interesting — they said it made them think about You and made them concerned about me, particularly about my tiredness.

I said, "You should read the last six weeks if You thought I was tired last year!"

But more seriously, I suppose I do sound tired, in part because I write in the morning when I'm still struggling to wake up (if I don't pray to You then, the chances of doing so go down dramatically) and in part because, well, I *am* tired.

That goes with being human, doesn't it? And growing older? And working hard?

I am touched by my friends' affection for me after all these years and for their fresh view of me and my character and personality. They are right. I need more rest. I should slow down a little.

Maybe I have already started. Maybe the pneumonia is a blessing in disguise because it will force me to do so for at least a while.

December 17, 1990 — Chicago

While I was reading the psalm this morning — and sniffling and sneezing — I was momentarily taken by a sense of how much You love each one of us. It was a brief experience that made me weep — even if my sneezing had already produced tears. You have a mother's love for the dope addict, the woman living on a machine for four years, the kid killed yesterday in a fight over a sports jacket, the homeless person who will not go to a shelter even when one is offered, the mugger lying in wait for a victim, the overweight person hardly able to walk, the Iraqi soldier waiting in his trench, the Russian soldier living as a refugee for all practical purposes in East Germany, the baby killed in an auto accident.

You love each of us with a unique and special love, a full-time task one would think even for God. You suffer when each of us suffers, an enormous amount of suffering. You are vulnerable and fragile with our vulnerability and fragility, a vast weakness. Only God could possibly stand it.

I sense overwhelming, vulnerable, suffering love on this week before Christmas, and while the skies grow dark and the *Messiah* plays on my CD I believe in that love. Either You are that way or You are not and the second option is inconceivable. Help me to understand better Your love and live in the palm of Your hand.

December 18, 1990 — Chicago

Another morning of grayness and drizzle, now just a week before Christmas. The Christmas spirit is still hard to come by. I love You. Help me to love You more and to celebrate this joyous season joyously.

December 19, 1990 — Chicago

My Love,

Tomorrow I have another chest X-ray. To judge by my general state of well-being, my lungs will be clear. Grant that it might be so.

In the Acts this morning Paul and Barnabas set out on their first missionary journey, a decisive step for Christianity. I wonder if they really understood the whole scope of what they were teaching. Even two millennia later, do we even now understand what Your son Jesus was all about?

Yet it somehow seemed easier then, or so I thought as I read the passage of Acts. Not physically easier. Jet lag was trivial compared to what they suffered on their travels, to say nothing of the risk of prison, torture, and death. But the message was clear, the goals were clear, the opposition was clear.

While they had to spend some of their time fighting their own, they didn't have a mammoth and corrupt institutional Church with which to contend.

Well, even if it was simpler then, I live now, not then, and I must contend with the conflicts of my own situation. I often wonder how I got myself so far out on the margins. I guess I can trace it out through a number of influences. I might say I went to the margin convinced that I had support behind me, and then it disappeared and I had no choice but to live a marginal life.

I'm sure my work is important and it affects a great number of people. Yet it was never what I intended... but that's silly, isn't it? It's what You intended. Anyway I love You and I trust You and I beg You to continue to care for me.

December 21, 1990 — Chicago

My Love,

I'm going crazy! Two faxes before I got up this morning, a Federal Express as I was getting out of bed, and the phone ringing incessantly all day. So, with all the stuff happening, I got to this reflection six hours late.

Today, tomorrow, and Sunday are all going to be mad. Maybe on Christmas Day, when all I have to do this year is say the kids' Mass at St. Mary of the Lake, I'll have some time to pray.

It's a dark gloomy day. I can't even see the buildings across the street. I don't like my new novel, although the publishers are very happy with it. I don't like any of the novels at this phase, however.

But I'm still alive and apparently not dying according to the X-ray yesterday, which shows whatever the thing was in my lung is breaking up — and with air holes (bronchial tubes I guess) in it, which doesn't happen with a tumor.

I really intended yesterday to come home and call up these reflections to express my gratitude. But there was not a second of time and I ran late for the rest of the day. I'm sorry I couldn't squeeze in a minute to say proper thanks till my very quick nighttime prayers. I let prayer and swimming, two of the most important activities in my life, get squeezed out by the phone and similar demands.

The lung isn't cleansed yet, though it surely is clearing. More X-rays in two weeks. But there is not much to worry about now, which doesn't mean that I won't worry a little bit anyway, just so I can continue to be Irish, which is to say continue to be human.

Anyway, thank You very much for taking care of me and giving me longer life. Help me to use that life well in Your service.

Help me, too, to find some time these next couple of days to pray.

Off to the mayor's for dinner, which is very nice indeed. At least someone in the city likes me, if not in the archdiocese! Oh, You know what I mean!

December 22, 1990 — Chicago

My Love,

An example of what happens to my time: last *Sunday* I noted that I needed more aspirin of the kind I take every day as a preventive for heart attacks. Last night (*Friday*) at 11:30 after I came home from Mayor Daley's I finally had an opportunity to walk the block to Walgreen's to make the purchase! That is absurd. But it's an accurate picture of how time is eaten up this week and of why it has been impossible to reflect at any great length. The situation is not helped by my postpneumonia weariness and depression. Nor by the huge meals that are shoved in front of me and that I must eat. I am tired, depressed, harassed, frustrated, and discouraged. I need to get to Tucson and away from everyone and everything.

But this is an awful way to feel during the joyous season!

Moreover, it's turning bitter cold and snow is expected. I have three visits today, Mass, and two visits tomorrow, an early morning TV and Mass on Christmas Eve, and three visits on Christmas Day!

I know You know all these things, but I also know that You want to hear from me just as every lover does.

I am a little better this morning after a good night's sleep, but the thought of the next four days already makes me feel hassled and hurried.

Help me, please!

December 23, 1990 — Chicago

My Love,

I'm tired and depressed. I feel like I've had a relapse of the pneumonia (or maybe even something worse from that mysterious area in my lung), but more likely I'm not getting enough sleep and, although I'm convalescent, I'm trying to keep up the usual Christmas pace. I have two parties I must go to tonight and then I have to be up at 5:30 to make a CBS broadcast tomorrow morning. Maybe tomorrow with some sleep after the program and a chance to pray I'll catch up with Christmas. I seem to be playing catch-up all the time. It's this way every Christmas, but worse this year when I'm not myself yet.

I guess I'm discouraged about my health. After almost seven weeks I wonder whether I'll ever be completely well.

That's silly and I know it is, but one must be honest with lovers.

Give me my health back, if it be Your will, as soon as possible.

December 24, 1990 — Chicago

Christmas Eve and I'm rushing. The morning has gone down the drain with cleaning up the house. I still must do my swim and then maybe I'll get time to reflect.

I do have two ideas on which I want to ponder. The first is that the rush of Christmas visits is in fact a continuous act of love and that the love involved may be more important than my own selfish reflections. Odd, I feel guilty about missing the reflections, I really do, and I take little or no spiritual comfort from the visiting and the partying, which are acts of love for You and in Your name. I'll try to spend time reflecting too, but I'll also try to be more celebratory at the parties.

Secondly, I continue to expect from myself what I would have done last year, even though I'm struggling back from sickness. I am not nearly as patient or as tolerant of myself as I should be — and, as You well know, I am terribly upset about the slow pace of recovery.

I even wonder, as again You know, whether I'm suffering a setback or whether it's only a lack of the kind of sleep I need. Mostly the latter, I think. Combined with a rush to health which was premature.

Although I know that whatever it is in my lung is breaking up and that there are no airholes in a tumor, I have been so depressed the last couple of days that I have again become fatalistically convinced that I have only a short time left.

It is surely the case that none of us have a very long time and that there is a remote chance of wrong diagnosis. But that's the depression talking. I guess I have to be patient with that too.

And I love You very much.

Thank You for everything.

December 25, 1990 — Chicago

My Love,

I feel renewed on this feast of renewal, though in truth more renewed by nine hours' sleep last night. It's clear that sleep is the answer to my weariness and depression. I feel fine today after two hours in the morning and nine hours last night.

But today is a splendid, wonderful feast of lights and color and gifts and carols and little children. The Mass at St. Mary's yesterday was wonderful, if a little loud. This will be a busy day for me and I kind of dread its rush, especially in this cold weather with its slippery streets. I must realize that my visits are acts of love and make them so to the best of my ability.

I am not, in all truth, on the upswing. This past year has not been a good year — the deaths and illness of friends, the failures, the pneumonia.

I feel, how shall I say, weakened, on the downturn, spent, at the end of my rope, as if my contribution has been made and the forces of decline and destruction are closing in.

If there are trajectories in life, and I think there are, my trajectory seems to be on the way down.

That may well not be true. It may be the pneumonia talking — and its "Great Depression." It's only long after events are over that one can see the trajectories. And, in any case, as I should be thinking today, there is one trajectory that is always up, that of Your love for me, incarnated so powerfully in the crib scene and in the wonder that shines in children's eyes. I believe that is the ultimate symbol of what the universe is all about. Even if I am not here next Christmas, I will still celebrate it even more wondrously in the kingdom of Your love.

December 26, 1990 — Chicago

My Love,

A lot of poignancy touches my soul on this Boxing Day. "The Tinker's Wife" in my Irish poetry reading this morning, a dream about Christ the King last night (along with swimming in a warm Lake Michigan in June), and thoughts of old friends now celebrating their first divorced Christmas. And more generally the ephemeral nature of human hopes and desires and expectations — not so much in a melancholy way as with a quiet sadness. A sadness, however, which does not believe that all that is good and loving and beautiful need ever end. It is at least preserved in You and that is all that matters.

I guess I'll continue to dream about Christ the King even if I never return there. Maybe it's good that I will not return, maybe the dream would have turned into a nightmare. Have I not learned yet that You know better than I about the trajectories of my life? Why fight the Spirit, as I always say.

Yesterday was a good day, one of the better Christmases in recent years because I was not as tired as I have been recently. The extra sleep which pneumonia imposes on me makes me feel better till the end of the day when I tend to collapse as I did last night.

The dream about the warm waters of Lake Michigan was clearly a reference to my hunger to get to Arizona. I'm going to try to get back to remembering dreams as I did last summer (all now lost in a hard disk error, though You remember them). It was a useful form of self-knowledge.

I feel like an exile today, part of all the poignancy. Not an unhappy exile, just a melancholy one.

Just the same, I love You and trust myself to You.

December 27, 1990 — Chicago

Only nine days away from Tucson. I've about finished my self-assigned sociology project for the year, so the last two months are not a complete wash. When I get to Tucson, I'll loaf for three weeks and devote February and March to the next novel. I hope I can force myself not to work for those three weeks.

I saw *Godfather III* yesterday. Not anti-Catholic at all as I thought it might be. Not as good as the first two, but still very good indeed.

Even in the "Outfit," you feel at the end of your life that you've failed.

In my prayer reading this morning I read that I am stone and clay until You make something out of me.

How true! And how readily forgotten! Although we humans know that we are transient beings we still sustain our illusion of independence, we kid ourselves into thinking that we are in charge when in fact we are totally dependent on You.

Who and what I am is because of the raw material You made me, what You willed I be instead of rock and stone. All my quickness, my facility with words and ideas, my industry are gifts You have given me. I have used them enthusiastically, You know, but never with the respect that they have deserved. Hence I find myself like the Godfather — toward the end of my life, tired, weary, and discouraged when I compare what I might have done with Your gifts and what I have in fact done.

I'm not a failure as I used to think, though I have failed at many things. But I am not what You wanted me to be either. In whatever time is left to me, help me to discover what that is and be it.

December 29, 1990 — Chicago

A rainy, humid, end-of-year morning during which I cleaned up the apartment (more or less, mostly less) and did laundry. Bear game this afternoon!

I'm still struck by the contrast between *Godfather III* and *Alice*, seen on the nights of the 27th and 28th, both of them with confession scenes (or rite of Christian reconciliation). In the former, confession did not make it possible to change, to begin again, while in the latter it did. Woody Allen was preaching quintessential Catholic doctrine, that you can begin again. He has become the outstanding Catholic propagandist of the era, from which it does not follow that Church leaders will recognize him as such.

It's a wonderful year-end reflection and indeed also wonderful for the Feast of the Holy Family, which means that I will preach it tomorrow at St. Mary's of the Woods and later at Our Mother of Sorrows in Tucson.

It is possible to begin again. It is hard and we never do it perfectly, but it can be done. I must begin again on the relaxation kick, now because I have no choice. I must begin again on joy and happiness, on forgiveness and peace, on gratitude and patience.

Help me to realize that Woody is right and Coppola is wrong. We are not fated to nothingness. Even if my life were to last merely another week, I would still be able to begin again.

I believe that. I love You. Help me to love You more.

December 30, 1990 — Chicago

My Love,

A sleepy Sunday afternoon. Snow falls lazily outside. I've loafed around since I came home from Mass two hours ago. I give up on trying to figure out my health. I'm better than I was a couple of weeks ago. But how much better? I continue to worry about my lungs though the doctors seem to think that the grounds for worry are over. I'm sorry for the preoccupation.

I was thinking as I drove to and from Mass how much I want to win, how much, that is, I want to be accepted by the institutions that don't want me, the diocese and the university, and how much I want my books to be hailed by those who dismiss them, whether they be the critics or clergy and hierarchy.

These are absurd wishes. I thought I had both of them under control but obviously I did not. The combination of my loss at Christ the King and the loss at the university at the end of this year have depressed me more than is proper — though of course the remnants of pneumonia create a depression-prone context.

In any case, I can't have it both ways. I can't play an outsider's game and expect to be accepted as an insider. I kid myself into thinking that this is going to change and of course it's not. What is surprising is that I'm something of an insider in the city, a role that doesn't make any difference.

I'm sad, I guess, because at the tag end of life, so many dreams have not come true. Stupidly I don't face the fact that dreams I never dared to dream have also come true. There have been prices to be paid, but they are small in comparison to what has happened.

The really foolish thing is not to trust You, to worry about foolish worries and foolish lost causes when You have taken care of me so well through the years.

So today, once again, at year's end I commit myself in trust to You and promise to try to dismiss foolish worries.

I love You.

December 31, 1990 — Chicago

I thank You for the return of the sun and light as well as the Light You have brought into the world. Just as the sun exorcises the clouds and the darkness and the mist and the fog, so may the Light of the world clear the fog out of my head.

I thank You for the graces of the year, for my family and my friends, for the intensification of love, for the good reviews, for the warm receptions to my lectures, for the achievements of my research, for my new publisher, for the return of my health, for the summer fun, for the parishes at which I work, for my articles and books, for those who have helped me, for the continuation of my faith, for sustaining my life, for protecting me from more serious harm, and for all the other good things with which You have blessed me.

Protect me and take care of me, help me to relax and be happy during the year that starts tonight. Help me to love You more and more.

January 1, 1991 — Chicago

I just talked to Bishop Clete O'Donnell to wish him a happy New Year. He sounded a little glum and discouraged. I got him to laugh and his voice picked up. Part of the problem is diabetes, but most of it is discouragement over the state of the Church — a valid discouragement if there ever was one.

In a properly run Church he'd be a cardinal. Well, no one ever said that You'd guarantee that the Church would be properly run. Take care of him. He's a great one.

I swam three-quarters of a mile this morning, with no appreciable ill effects, so I guess I'm over the pneumonia. Now, if it be Your will and my lung is clear or even clearer tomorrow, that incident in my life will be finished. It was not pleasant but I thank You again and again and again for making me get off that plane in L.A.

It's enough to confirm my faith in angels. I'm sure an angel dragged me off the plane.

So I face the new year, one less year in my life than a year ago, with recovering health, some disappointments, some successes, and the usual mystery of what, as my niece Eileen Durkin said long ago, I'm going to be when I grow up. Take care of me and protect me during the year to come, help me to live as You want me to live and to be more the person You want me to be.

January 2, 1991 — Chicago

My Love,

Well, I lost most of today's reflection because of keyboard error. But You heard it. I said that it would be better to accept my fears of the test today, as irrational as they may be, as part of my ordinary humanity instead of pretending that they don't exist or being harsh on myself for their irrationality. Any brush with mortality is bound to be scary, particularly to one with an imagination as active as mine. I should acknowledge and accept my fear instead of trying to repress it or reject it.

Nonetheless, I beg You, in all the fear of my own fragility, grant that I may be well today and that this test business might finally come to an end. Whatever happens, I will always love You.

January 3, 1991 — Chicago

Well, I am fully prepared and ready to go to Tucson. My lungs are fine (the "irritation" is fading), and my teeth are fine, and my apartment is clean. I have no assignments for the next three weeks save for rest.

I'll work on the novel in February and on the International Social Survey Program in March as my assignments for the coming semester and perhaps spend two weeks in Ireland, maybe with a trip to Rome, in May — You willing, naturally.

As You can tell, knowing me as You do, I am now really in the euphoria of health and hope. I will not, however, again with Your help, permit that euphoria to interfere with the three weeks of rest that I so desperately need.

Thank You for bringing me through the pneumonia relatively unscathed and for protecting my immune system from worse troubles. The only remaining aftereffect is the extra weight — and all my problems should be that minor. It's been a difficult autumn, part of the human condition. I'm glad I'm bouncing back and I'm grateful I have a place like Tucson to run to.

Thank You too for all the beauty in the world — yesterday the poinsettia exhibit at the park, the music of *Carmen* and the Christmas tree in the Daley Center at night.

Let there be peace in the Persian Gulf.

January 5, 1991 — Somewhere over Texas

My Love,

In the air three hours late on the way to Tucson. People on the plane are very impatient because of the delay, apparently expecting on-time service despite six inches of Chicago snow. Maybe I've begun to relax, but I am being philosophical about it, a new reaction for me. Not so many years ago a storm like this one would have closed everything down, and not too many years before that it would be a two-day train ride to Tucson and not too many years before that several months of animal riding.

We don't know how good we have it!

The party last night was a huge success, best of my Epiphany parties yet, complete with my contemporaries and my niece and Mrs. Brennan singing. If we could have persuaded one of the teens, Beth or Brigid, to sing we would have had four generations.

Thank You for the friends, for the opportunity to entertain them, and for this trip to Tucson, so desperately needed at the present. I love You.

January 7, 1991 — Tucson

My Love,

Looks like a sunny day, for which many, many thanks.

I'm reading in Acts about St. Paul's travels and I marvel at the sheer physical energy and strength it took to make those journeys. Or the journeys of my immigrant ancestors. Or of the great explorers. And one six-hour flight to Tucson via Phoenix wears me out. I'm tempted to call myself a softy. In truth I would not have lasted long on those earlier journeys. You did not design me for travel.

The two poems I read this morning are about the frailty of human life, a frailty which we try to dodge though its truth lurks at the limits of our imagination, haunting us. The poet's function is, among other things, to warn us. My novels, my sociology, all my concerns and worries are as transient as yesterday.

I'm going to try some of my own poetry in the next few days, once I get a little energy back, but for the moment I'm going to do nothing more than loaf.

I love You.

January 8, 1991 — Tucson

My Love,

I was up at 4:45 this morning to go over to station KGUN for a "Good Morning America" interview about Pope John Paul I's death, new interest having been stirred up by *Godfather III*. The interview went well enough. I hope my love for Catholicism as well as my ambivalence about the Vatican showed through.

It's only a week before the war deadline in the Persian Gulf. Please, PLEASE prevent war! Most Americans really do not want it, but we're at the mercy of our leaders. I have been outspoken in my columns on the subject, which is about all I can do. I will continue to attack the war if it should come, though that's no great heroism on my part, only simple morality.

One of the poems I read this morning is about the change from the 1960s to the 1970s, exaggerated no doubt, but still an interesting object lesson in how culture patterns which seem to be new and exciting and inevitable can prove to be transient and dull. The mood of the poem is that life goes on and human hopes die. There is an element of truth in this grim reading of reality; in the novel I'm working on now, one of the group of five kids who started together in first grade (the most appealing) is dead, one is in jail, and two are on the way to alcoholism. Only one survives, the least idealistic and the most pragmatic of the lot.

Yet that is not all that is to be said, not by a long shot. Even my protagonist, pragmatist that he is, continues to *hope*. In fact his hope is stronger than his pragmatism. Not everything need deteriorate permanently. Even death in the end is a loser.

This I do believe, though sometimes it is hard to do so.

I love You, and I believe Your promise of victory over death.

January 9, 1991 — Tucson

My Love,

The meeting for peace being held in Geneva goes on. Grant that there might be peace.

War is so foolish, horrible, and unnecessary.

The poem today was a vivid description of a band concert at Fullham Palace on the Thames — and the poet's fears about the nuclear bomb wiping out all the beauty. It's a political poem because the poet, an academic, shows the typical academic obsession with the bomb, an obsession which now seems to have been foolish — though the presence of those things still in the world is enough to cause some worry in anyone.

But curiously or perhaps not so curiously his thoughts do not turn to any ultimate issue besides the end of an autumn afternoon, neither to the fact that even if there is no bomb, all those at Fullham Palace that day will die anyway, nor to the fact that where there is so much beauty there must also be Beauty, or at least there may be Beauty.

He did not, in other words, ask about You — which seems to me to have missed the point. If You *are*, and if You are Love, then the beauty of that afternoon is something which will transcend death no matter what causes death. You are apparently not an issue any more.

I read Richard Kearney's book *The Wake of the Imagination* about postmodernism yesterday, a movement which represents the ultimate in nihilistic despair — not only have You disappeared; so too has "Man," nothing is left at all. Even without the bomb the world disintegrates. No more stories, no more imagination, no more anything.

Which, as Kearney points out in refutation, is itself a highly imaginative story.

If there is a story then there must be a storyteller, or even a Storyteller. The thing that would be hard to believe, it seems to me, is that all the lives that afternoon at Fullham Palace were a story, each its own story, each a story of a love affair with You.

But if I find that difficult to believe, the reason is that I don't know You well enough yet. It is in Your nature, should You exist at all, to be capable of millions, billions of stories at the same time. Some trick!

January 10, 1991 — Tucson

The news from Geneva yesterday was terrible. Apparently Mr. Bush will get the war he wanted. God help us all, that is to say,

You help us all. Still I wouldn't be surprised if something turns up which gives Iraq a chance to back off before next Tuesday. Grant that it be so.

I saw the movie *Ghost* last night, six months late. It's an example of how the critics, not liking or understanding religion, kept me away from an excellent religious film about heaven, hell, and purgatory. I think Roger Ebert was out of town and didn't review it. He would have comprehended what it was about. Fortunately word of mouth overcame the critics. I figured I ought to see it because any film that remains in theaters for six months must be an interesting film on some level.

It certainly raised the question of faith and of life after death, of human survival, in a powerful and graphic way. Some (agnostic or atheist) critics have raised the question of whether the writer and the director are cynically manipulating the audience with hints of survival in which they themselves do not believe. Surely it is a sweet and entertaining, even sentimental story. But sweetness and sentimentality are not evil. Nor has it ever been written that films must not be entertaining. The issue, it seems to me, is not whether the filmmakers are cynical but whether the film does make one think about the meaning of life and the possibility that You might be that benign and gracious light that comes down to absorb Patrick Swayze at the end of the film.

I think You are. I believe that You are Light and Love and that You will triumph eventually not only over death but over cynicism too.

January 11, 1991 — Tucson

My Love,

The war draws closer. Thank You that some United States Congressmen (including my friend Pat Moynihan) have the courage to stand up and say "no." And the Churches this time too, even [Cardinal] Joe Bernardin on Chicago TV with his damn French cuffs. Please, please turn the hearts of the two men involved — Bush and Hussein — and prevent war! Please grant us peace!

January 13, 1991 — Tucson

My Love,

It looks very much like there is going to be war. My hopeful prediction that Saddam Hussein would act rationally even if George Bush might not seems to have been wrong. There are still two days left. Perhaps something can yet be accomplished in the cause of peace. Grant that it may be so.

Oh, how blind men of power can be!

Stop it if You possibly can, I beg You!

I'm sorry, but that is the only prayer I can utter on this brilliant Sunday afternoon in Arizona.

I also wish to pray for the families of those who have men and women in the Persian Gulf and for those Iraqi families with fighting men about whom they are as worried as are the families of American service persons.

January 14, 1991 — Tucson

My Love,

A return to tyranny and the Big Lie in Lithuania and war drawing near in the Persian Gulf: what a terrible way to begin a new year and what a terrible reversal of the hopes of a year ago. The world is much less than a perfect place. I guess I knew that, but the astonishing changes of the past year made me expect more.

Just as the Vatican Council had led me to expect more.

I pray for the Lithuanians, especially those who are dying. I pray for all those in the Persian Gulf who will die. I pray for peace. What more can be said?

Yesterday's psalm, the lament of the exiles in Babylon (calling to mind Verdi's superb chorus) remains poignant every time I read it. Unlike so many psalms, it rings true to my own experience, not only as an exile from my archdiocese and university but also, and more important, as an exile from my real home, which I do believe is with You, my true Love.

January 15, 1991 — Tucson

My Love,

This is the day war begins again. The day freedom seems to die in Russia. I don't want to think about such things. Dear God, please help and protect all the people involved.

David in the psalm this morning talks about protection from enemies. As the full story of the violation of my private papers slowly emerges I know more deeply than ever what enemies are — and how driven and obsessed to the point of irrationality by hatred they can be. It is this kind of obsessive hatred in the leaders of the U.S. and Iraq and in the old guard in Moscow which has brought about the present crises. Is there nothing the rest of us can do to chain the furies of such twisted people? If there is, we haven't found out about it yet.

Maybe the best way to stop war is to have elections in both countries, referenda on a war. Give the people a vote, not their power-drunk leaders.

Once again I pray for peace. Please, please grant that even at the last minute it won't be too late.

January 16, 1991 — Tucson

My Love,

I'm reading the poems of the Polish poet Czeslaw Milosz. He's at Berkeley now, as the poet Seamus Heaney is at Harvard, which says something interesting about the distribution of poets in the world. He is wonderfully Catholic and captures the poignancy of life as well as its unquenchable instinct of hope. Just like the Greg Bear novel I read last night, his poems believe in purpose and that nothing is ever lost. Bear sees it going into the "Final Mind," a nice touch of Aquinas's Final Cause. Shags [theologian John Shea] made the same observation, perhaps quoting one of the process theologians, a couple of years ago. All those events and persons which cause a sharp dagger of poignant memory to plunge into the heart, all those visions of childhood and young adulthood which are so sweet as to make one cry, all these survive in the mind of God and with them we too survive.

Bear has a powerful Catholic imagination. I don't know whether he deliberately makes the Final Mind a mix of Thomism and process theology or whether it is an unconscious effect. But it is quite vivid. I'm not sure You act quite that way, but who knows how You act. Anyway, it is a great metaphor.

I'm doing better at remembering You during the day, now that I have put my keys on the top of Our Lady of Guadalupe. Thanks for the idea. Help me to keep at it.

No war yet. Russia is making a last desperate bid. May it work. *Please.*

I love You.

January 17, 1991 — Tucson

My Love,

The war started last night. So far we seem to be winning quickly and cheaply, if war can ever be cheap. Having lived through four wars I am skeptical of early and optimistic claims. The big advantage of a quick victory will be that on neither side will the casualties be as horrendous as they might. I do not identify our side with moral right. But the other side is far worse than we are. However, I pray for a quick war so that many people will be spared pain and loss. Grant that there be peace. I love You.

January 18, 1991 — Tucson

My Love,

War continues. Missiles fell on Israel last night. End it soon, please.

Milosz's poetry continues to be breathtaking — an old man (five years later he is still alive and writing for the Op Ed pages of the *Times*, one tough Pole) mourning for his wife and his mother and his father, mourning but also with a sense of hope.

My parents are dim figures for me now, my mother obscured by her last days of diabetes and Alzheimer's, as we call it now, my father a driven man, riding the streetcar to work, three and a half hours back and forth to his office on the South Side. The memories before that are of the Depression, memories with which, for all my efforts, I am unable to cope. Yet I loved them deeply and still miss them in my dreams. Somehow I feel that I was distant from them even then. I don't quite understand it. Maybe my grades and my bookishness established a barrier behind which I retreated. They were, however, proud of me and I'm sure that my values are their values.

We were, God (You) know(s), not much given to displays of affection, which may have meant that the love was all cooped up inside us, seeping out indeed and having its effect, but indirectly.

Should I try to go back and recover some of that era with self-hypnotism? Is there any point in it? I suppose there is. More understanding of self — and perhaps of my angers. I wonder if I should try to recapture more of that. Why not?

January 19, 1991 — Tucson

My Love,

The war goes on, apparently with considerable success. Someone on the TV said that there was a fifty-fifty chance of a ground war. Please don't let that happen.

Death is much on my mind these days, partly because of Milosz's wonderful poetry, partly because I have decided to order things for my own death (not so much because I was sick with pneumonia), partly because I have read a commentary on the funeral liturgy, and partly because there have been so many deaths among my friends recently.

However, Milosz's poem this morning was about heaven, which he claimed to have seen among flowers on a riverbank. He believes in heaven, but he wonders if there will be day and night and seasons and even mortality, which means so much in our psyche. He admits that it is impossible to figure it out.

What comes next? Like every Christian since the time of Jesus I believe that life continues — in the mind of God or the "Final Mind" of Bear's novel. I suppose like every Christian I have wondered what it will be like. Dante has one poetic vision, Milosz another. In a sense I vote with the Pole instead of the Italian. It will be like what we know here, like a bank of flowers along the river, only much better. Perhaps even a great city by a lake, like Chicago without the problems! I love You.

January 20, 1991 — Tucson

Milosz's poem this morning is about one of my favorite subjects — angels! Imagine a Nobel Prize poet writing about angels. I hardly need add that Milosz's Catholicism is barely noticed in this country. Poets are even less important to the American Church than novelists.

Anyway, he wonders what the angels think of us, how they must be baffled by our materiality (we can feel human hair, he says, as we caress it) and our mortality. He is not ready to give either of these up in a trade with the angels.

What indeed do these beings think of us? I believe in them, as You well know, not as a matter of faith but as a matter of aesthetics. Was it Bonaventure who said that if angels are possible, they exist? I like that argument. I'd be disappointed if there were not angels somewhere in creation. As I wrote in *Angel Fire,* there has to be someone like my heroine Gabriella somewhere in creation.

But what do these beings think of us? The character Desmond protests that Gabriella likes humans the way we like wolfhounds — nice doggy!

She denies it and I believe her. And I disagree, with all due respect, with Milosz. They don't envy us and they don't view us with puzzled contempt. They love us because it is in their nature to love. What is unbodied love like? Less passionate? As I tried to say in the story, it is more passionate rather than less. Just as Your Love is the most passionate of all! Angels are beings which reflect even more clearly than we do Your passionate love.

Much interest in them these days, a whole table at Rizzoli's bookstore, creatures of wonder and surprise and astonishment reflecting a universe of wonder and surprise and astonishment — an exciting vision on this desert Sunday morning when the war goes on. Despite all the agony, there is always surprise.

I love You and I adore Your surprises!

January 21, 1991 — Tucson

My Love,

Milosz's poems continue to move on. His mother died after the war after caring for an old German woman who was sick with typhus. That kind of example would surely give one both a deep sense of faith and a powerful awareness of tragedy. He believes in You, no doubt about that, but he also wonders about the misery and suffering in the world. How can this be if You are really Love?

A fair question which I often ask and which I ask again as this war grows more terrible and more people die. A fair question indeed but one to which there is no ready answer. Why must we suffer, why must we die, why must there be so much cruelty and misery and evil? Why all the envy and hatred?

I don't understand these things and on these gray days out here, still affected, I suppose by the remnants of pneumonia and tired from my fast, I find that I become melancholy again. I think of all the things I have worked for and how badly most of them have failed. So much of the hopes of a quarter century ago wiped out. Admittedly I am not a failure as I used to think I was. Most people would laugh if they heard me say that I've lost most of the time. But they fail to understand how little celebrity and novelistic success mean to me and how much I still mourn the losses to men and women in my old group and the decline of the archdiocese.

So many senselessly ruined lives!

What can be said about all these events and tragedies?

Not much. They don't compare to the ugliness and horror of war. Yet the lives are ruined and they are lives of people I loved.

Grim today, huh? What can I tell You?

It's how I feel on this gloomy Monday

Let there be peace and perhaps even more happiness. I thank You for all the good. I love You.

January 22, 1991 — Tucson

My Love,

I continue to be fascinated by Milosz's poetry. In his "Six Lectures," he tries to explain what it was like in Poland and Lithuania between the wars, a world he knew as a young man. How can he describe, he asks his young students, the way that world, soon to be destroyed, seems to him in retrospect? Lovely, graceful images from the past, a past soon to be blotted out by catastrophe. A grace never to be restored.

There was nothing particularly unique in that world. It looks special in retrospect because it was destroyed, and all that remains are the images in the mind of a relatively few. Were they guilty? Is he guilty for not having prevented the destruction? Is everyone guilty? If everyone is guilty, is no one guilty?

I don't know how to explain the holocausts of 1939 to 1945. Milosz thinks that Jesus must forgive everyone. There was little the ordinary people, the people in his images, could have done to prevent the war. The Nazis never had a majority in a German election.

But what about American responsibility for the deaths in the Persian Gulf? Currently a majority of the people back the president. Does that not make them responsible for this ugly and unnecessary war? A majority did not support it before it happened. I presume a majority will oppose it again soon. Moreover, the cause is just even if the war is unnecessary. Could our era be wiped out by it as Milosz's was? I rather doubt it, not even in the way the Vietnam War wiped out the post-1945 era in this country. But I worry about all the prices that will be paid for Mr. Bush's war.*

I also remember the Christ the King era in my young adulthood, doubtless magnified in importance by my selective memories. In reality it was not all that great, I suppose. In my dreams last night, for reasons that escape me, I returned to that era and met some of the people again — this time even winning a few of the causes I lost!

Admittedly their lives were not wiped out by war. But many of them destroyed themselves anyway, not to the point of actual suicide so much as the slow suicide of drink and self-punishment. As a young priest I had silly illusions about how much of this could be prevented. However, even if I had the wisdom and experience I do now, I would still have tried, perhaps more prudently, though no more successfully.

So I share Milosz's bafflement: why do so many things go wrong?

I guess I'm stuck with this answer: Jesus forgives!

That answer, and Your love.

---

* *Editor's note:* Out of his daily reflections on the Persian Gulf War, which continue in this book, Andrew Greeley eventually wrote a highly praised article in *The Critic* magazine summing up his strong — and evolving — feelings and thoughts. That article is reprinted at the end of this book.

January 23, 1991 — Tucson

My Love,

The war goes on and I continue to read Czeslaw Milosz's efforts to come to terms with *the* War, a catastrophe far worse than this one. Four wars in my generation — all of them at a great distance, even this, though one sees it in on TV every day. How ugly, how terrible, how senseless, how destructive war is!

And what a proof of original sin, or whatever we choose to call our flawed human nature today. All soldiers anywhere wish to do is to go home. The carnage is caused by a few leaders, caught up in their own power lust. Dreadful, simply dreadful! Even in a country like ours where there are democratic processes, a single man can still plunge us into war. What can be done now except to pray that somehow it will be short and that not too many people will die.

But those who launched the war about whose destructiveness Milosz agonizes *thought* it would be short.

I continue to dream about my past. Our dreams are as transient as our lives. When I was a young priest I knew I would learn only by mistakes and prayed for those who would be hurt by my mistakes. My mistakes didn't doom them, but I grieve that I was unable to save them, though my dreams of saving them were naive and foolish and perhaps even presumptuous.

As I said yesterday, those lives are blighted just like those about whom Milosz writes, though more slowly. Dear God, please help them and please forgive me for whatever mistakes my enthusiasms led me to make.

And end the war soon, please.

January 24, 1991 — Tucson

My Love,

The war is a week old and my guess is that it is not going as well as our leaders expected. My pessimism before it started seems justified. A lot of people are going to die, needlessly, senselessly. I think the media are catching on to it, and soon the people will, and soon after that the war will become very unpopular. How terrible it all is!

The three weeks here are almost over. I feel fine though not as relaxed as I might be. Still it has been good. I dread the two weeks in Chicago with all the lunches and suppers and the trips to Washington and New York. I don't want to undo the success of this rest. It will also be cold, something I have missed very little out here. And there will be an increase in danger in my five airplane flights because of the terrorist threat, not that I would consider staying off planes. I am in Your hands, protected under the shadow of Your wings. If You want to call me home, You'll do that.

Anyway, thank You for this period of rest and rehabilitation. Also once again thanks for this Arizona alternative life which I have enjoyed now for twelve years. I did not seek it and on my own would never have found desert warmth in the winter. When the University of Arizona decided that it wanted me, I didn't think much about winter warmth. Now, however, I am very grateful for it. As I am grateful for my increase in prayers out here. This afternoon, finally, I shall turn to that mode of thought which is best of all for reflection, poetry.

January 26, 1991 — Tucson

My Love,

Milosz's poetry makes me want to review my life. I'm used to saying, as You well know, that I think of my life as failure. And then I ask: How can anyone with twenty million books in print really be a failure? I don't argue any more because having all those books in print was never one of my goals, never even one of my wildest dreams. It was not a direction in which I particularly wanted to go. Nor did I ever much care about or even think about appearing on news programs or about being a celebrity. These things were orthogonal to my dreams and goals. I wanted to be a good parish priest and a sociologist in the service of the Church. The latter was a total washout. The former? I am still painfully aware of my mistakes and blunders at Christ the King, my substitution of enthusiasm, sometimes manic enthusiasm, for experience and even common sense. My subsequent attempt to create an informal parish community at Grand Beach was a disaster from which I probably will never recover. And my efforts to protect the members of that community from ruining their lives were also miserable failures. As I think about these events, vivid images of my blunders flash across my mind. I'm sorry for my mistakes and misjudgments and sins. I suppose that I often tried the impossible, rushed into situations in which a wiser and more prudent priest would never have tried to intervene. If I had it to do over — and of course I don't — I would be more circumspect.

So I still think I'm a failure — at what I wanted to do, if not at what You want me to do.

That's the dilemma of making sense out of my life now. I resolve it as You know by saying that You're the one who made up the game plan, an appropriate term on the eve of Super Sunday, and that there's no point in fighting the Holy Spirit because She doesn't like it. So maybe I can settle the question by saying that I have failed but You haven't.

Yet I have made terrible mistakes, some of them excusable perhaps, some not. You'll have to decide which are excusable. I'm sorry for all of them.

As for a sociologist in service of the Church, I am surely that, if not for the institutional Church. Again You knew what You were doing, even if I didn't.

A strange review. I'm sorry, it's the best I can do. Ambiguous as always.

January 27, 1991 — Tucson

My Love,

I've been reading Greg Bear's science fiction this week as well as Milosz's poetry. They have a remarkably similar theme — the search for meaning. Bear's protagonists are almost always searching for an explanation, a meaning in what has happened and is happening. They are pilgrims of the absolute. Similarly Milosz tries to find meaning in the tragedies and adventures of his life. Neither quest is perfectly satisfying, though Bear's protagonists find some clarification and Milosz by the very act of writing poetry imposes some meaning on the confusion of reality. Both successes, however, are tenuous.

The two authors are both Catholic and sometimes fall back on explicitly Catholic rhetoric and imagery. It's almost as though about Catholicism they have no doubt but only about life having purpose — another tribute to the power of the Catholic imagination.

Now I have to confess, my Love, that I am not one of these pilgrims of the absolute. The characters in my stories — Blackie, Lar, Ace, Kevin — are empiricists like I am and worry much more about the proximate than the ultimate, about the contingent rather than the absolute. They do this because the absolute questions seem resolved. They accept the Catholic worldview implicitly. They believe in You and in human survival, though they may have doubts at times. They do not expend time and energy worrying about the mysteries You have cast around on all sides — terrible mysteries like this awful war. You have made us all different. There is no need for me to become a pilgrim of the absolute, even if that means I may be a more shallow person. The world needs pragmatists too as well as mystics, Seamus as well as Czeslaw.

Yet perhaps one of the reasons I am still not over the ill effects on the psyche of my illness is that absolute and ultimate questions linger, that I am asking myself not perhaps what life means but what *my* life has meant. The answer I came up with yesterday certainly suffices intellectually, yet....

Yet I think there is something more there that I ought to strive to understand, something that goes beyond the insights I acquired while working on my memoir (*Confessions of a Parish Priest*). Perhaps I ought to read last year's journal of reflections to get some hint at what it is. I may need it or find it useful in the years to come, such as they may be.

You've designed a role for me. It may be wise at this time in my life to try to understand it better.

I love You.

January 28, 1991 — Tucson

My Love,

I'm ready to return to Chicago at the end of these three relaxing weeks, notably lighter in weight, and notably better in health if not totally free from the emotional impact of pneumonia. For the first two I thank You, and the final I accept as part of the human condition.

Yesterday we spoke about the search for meaning, and I said that I didn't seem to be so obsessed with ultimate meaning, perhaps because I had always been so much a part of a believing, a meaning-giving community. I am grateful for that community which has freed me up for other matters, but I also have my own little search going on about which I must reflect in the days and weeks ahead. What drives me after all? I cite Your kingdom (or whatever we might call it), and I think that's true in part, but there are other energies at work, mostly altruistic, but then we understand that altruism is often self-seeking too — always a rational choice!

Anyway, as I prepare to dash off to the airport, I love You and I will continue to search. Help me to see more clearly.

January 29, 1991 — Chicago

My Love,

As always I have mixed emotions on returning to Chicago — delight in this city, happiness at being at my real home, dislike of the cold weather, and anticipated weariness at the pace of life which I face — two airplane trips, lunch every day while I'm here, and supper at least half the time. I'll have to exercise great discipline if I'm not going to put back on all the weight I lost in Tucson.

What a strange life I live — I'm not complaining. Quite the contrary, as You know from my recent reflections, I am very grateful for the Tucson interludes in my life. They have helped to protect health and sanity. But I'm still an odd kind of priest, on the margin and yet very much on the inside through my writings. I've got into this position, not by intent, but by doing the things I do and discovering, usually after the fact, that the institutional leadership and the clerical culture cannot tolerate those things. So much of what constitutes the ambience and the matrix of my life is unintended. I'm "neighborhood people" and I don't have a neighborhood. I'd like to, but not having one is the price I have to pay. I wander a lot and I don't like wandering, but again to do what I must do, it is necessary to wander.

What is my role? I guess I have to say that my role is to wander along the margins, doing that which I have been trained to do, following the instincts You have given me, and saying what I think needs to be said.

Not what I planned, but not intolerable either. So far the benefits far outweigh the costs, though I acknowledge the costs. Anyway, I thank You for everything and I beg You to help me to be faithful to my calling.

February 1991

February 3, 1991 — Chicago

My Love,

The mystery book is finished, thank You very much. Two weeks of work with all the other stuff. Now I can turn to the major novel, pretty close to my winter schedule.

I think it's a good story, but one never knows.

My sixty-third birthday party tonight will be a lot of fun, but I'll probably eat too much too. We celebrate a little early but that's all right too. Thank You very much for the sixty-three years. They have been exciting and rewarding. I am very grateful.

Especially for the friends, many of whom will be there tonight.

I love You very much. I'm sorry if I forgot You during the last few days with the book, but You know the way I have to work on a book, so I'm sure You understand. I'll be back tomorrow under considerably less pressure.

February 4, 1991 — Chicago

My Love,

The novel is done! Seventy thousand words in two weeks. Not something to be proud of perhaps, but that's the way I work. Anyway the burden is lifted, for which many thanks. I've been at the machine all day from early morning, revising and rewriting. A copy has gone off to my agent and another copy to the office. I like the story, but then I always do. I think it's a neat puzzle and a neat solution and a tender love story and Blackie is outrageous and the Ryan clan swarms as it usually does.

I'm off to Washington early in the morning, where I'll be for my birthday talking to the Catholic college and university presidents — and I must remember that I haven't packed the talk. How stupid can I get! Excuse me.

Well, I've packed it now. Wouldn't it have been something else for me to arrive in Washington for a talk for which I have given up my birthday and on which I've worked so hard and then not have the talk!

Well, thank You or the relevant guardian angel (who works for You) for reminding me.

June summed up the birthday party last night with the comment that I am a very lucky person.

Oh, boy, am I!

Such remarkable and loving friends and such a loyal and wonderful family. Few people in the world have such friends. I am truly blessed. I don't deserve them, but how good it is to have them. I am very grateful to them and to You.

Mayor Daley and Maggie stayed till the bitter end and enjoyed themselves immensely. What warms me is not that they are the first family of Chicago but that they're old friends who like me and happen to be the first family. I would have wanted them there regardless. We became friends when he was still a state senator. When [theologian] Jack Shea asked for comments, Rich Daley was the first one to speak. "Make sure he has an absentee ballot!" In my remarks I congratulated him on cancelling the election because I had seen so little on TV and in the papers.

It was a great party and again I am grateful to You for it. It shows that with Your help I have done some good things in my life and made some good friends. How wonderful!

Thank You very much.

I love You.

February 5, 1991 — Somewhere over Pennsylvania

My Love,

I'm on the plane about a half-hour out of Washington. Lucky for me the cab driver had his radio on at 5:30 this morning and I discovered that Midway was closed by fog. So I went to O'Hare and got out on a flight in the nick of time. For which, thanks.

Sixty-three years ago today I came into the world. First of all I want to thank You for my parents who are still alive for me in my dreams, if in conscious life I have pretty much forgotten them. They were good people who left me a religious and intellectual heritage — and perhaps a genetic ability with words — that have been priceless blessings in my life. They had hard lives, much harder than mine, and so many of their hopes and dreams were blighted, first by the Depression, then by bad health. I stand on their shoulders. I am so much of what I am because of them. I pray for them, though I'm sure they do not need my prayers. I look forward to seeing them again.

There can be no doubt that I have led a providential life, directed into trajectories by Your grace that I would not have anticipated and did not expect. If I have become a tool for Your plans, it was not, I confess, because I was an especially docile tool. Sometimes I wonder whether it might have been better if I had not spread my interest and activities so wide, if I had chosen to concentrate on one thing (as some priests protest that I should) instead of being priest and sociologist and novelist and journalist. However, I have followed gut instincts and tried to be many different things. I will not therefore be rated as a great novelist or a great sociologist or a great journalist. On the other hand, no one has done the sociology that I have done, my novels are always good reads and spread an explicit religious message in a way that no other novelist does.

So I am what I am, mostly because You have made me what I am and for that I have no regrets. I have made mistakes and blunders for which I am very sorry and ask Your forgiveness.

I am also grateful, as I said yesterday, for the friends You have sent me, good friends, loyal friends, loving friends. I have been unfortunate sometimes in thinking that some people were friends when they were not. I suppose that is still happening because I am constitutionally too trusting. However, there are still many, many friends. I don't know what I'd do without them.

Finally, this morning I thank You for Your love which thrust me into existence and sustains me in existence and guides and directs my life. If I have one request this morning it is that I become an ever more docile and supple tool for Your plans and goals.

I do indeed love You.

February 6, 1991 — Washington, D.C.

My Love,

I'm fidgeting on the plane at Washington National. O'Hare is closed because of fog. Midway is open but for some reason this Midway plane is not moving. We've been waiting for an hour and we've no indication when we're going to take off.

My patience with air travel, never great, is almost nonexistent. I am tired, irritable, discouraged, my temper on a hair trigger. This is almost entirely a physical reaction, but physical or emotional, it's awful. I don't sleep well in hotels, no matter how much sleep I get.

That talk last night was not, I think, a success — despite the work I put into it. Maybe my delivery was too fast, maybe there was too much crammed into it, or maybe I misread the reaction. Or perhaps I expect enthusiasm and agreement every time I open my Irish mouth.

Or maybe I'm still tired from the pneumonia.

As You can tell, I'm not in a good mood. I dread the New York trip next week when I'll be in a worse mood.

There's nothing much I can do about it, I fear, because it's almost all physical. Maybe I shouldn't be traveling yet, but I am and now I have to. Help me through this difficult time.

I love You.

Still no sign that they're going to let us take off.

February 8, 1991 — Chicago

My Love,

So tired, so really tired. As I knew it would, this interlude in Chicago, Washington, and New York has exhausted me. The ill effects of the pneumonia have yet to leave me. I conclude that on return to Tucson I have to get back into my vacation mode as I was in January — with ten pages of fiction a day and no more work than that. It would mean keeping my entertaining and social life to an absolute bare minimum. That will be hard. But the truth of the matter is that I knew even in January that I was still dragging.

Maybe tomorrow I'll be less weary. Help me at least to think of You during the day.

February 9, 1991 — Chicago

My Love,

I'm much better today, for which many thanks. A good night's sleep, a little bit of relaxation and reading, a chance for some reflection. It is amazing how quickly I can improve under those conditions.

I've read Irish poetry again this morning and a book on memory as storytelling, one that equates intelligence with the ability to tell the right story at the right time and in the right way. I must learn more about stories, especially humorous ones. I must also find some of those humor newsletters that I seem to have lost, when I get around to straightening up my apartment, which I was going to do this trip and never did. Hey, I just remembered where they were and found them!

I love You. Help me to persist in my present refreshed mode.

February 10, 1991 — Chicago

My Love,

I read Anna Quindlen's novel *Object Lessons* today. What a beautiful book it is, so much Catholic hope. And what a pity that the Church is oblivious to the flourishing of the Catholic imagination in this country.

I must return again to June's comment on my birthday — what a lucky person I am! Oh, yes, so lucky! I am very grateful indeed. Grant that my life may continue to demonstrate that hope.

I love You.

February 12, 1991 — Somewhere over Lake Michigan

My Love,

Off to New York on a clear morning with the promise of acceptable weather. I'm already tired and the trip has just begun. How much I hate traveling, and yet how much I love it. I look forward to the return to Tucson and (perhaps) more rest. At least no plane flights for six weeks.

Jack Durkin will need more surgery. I have the terrible feeling that this might be the end for him. Please, please grant that it is not.

We're over Lake Michigan now. Snow covers the beaches. It looks like the moon. But soon it will be summer again. How much I love summer and all it means! But summers go by too fast as does all time. Still I'm a terribly lucky person as I've tried to tell myself during these busy and exhausting and discouraging two weeks.

Overload again, I suppose. And more complaints. How tired You must be of hearing me say that I'm tired!

But You love me and hence You want to listen to me even when I complain.

I'm sorry. I do love You. Please help the Durkins.

February 13, 1991 — New York

My Love,

Lunch at the *New York Times* today, American Association for Public Opinion Research this afternoon, my literary agent at supper, "Today" show and twenty-five-city satellite tour tomorrow, and then the eight-hour flight back to Tucson via Dallas. It's a long way from St. Angela and from Christ the King. I ask myself what am I doing here with these projects and these concerns. Yet AAPOR and the *Times* are certainly important witness events as is the "Today" show, especially on the subject of marriage. At least according to the theories I learned as a seminarian and as a young priest, I belong here, doing what I'm doing. I am, furthermore, the only priest many of the folks will hear from one end of the year to the other. And I know the impact of the novels on people. So it is part of my vocation and a crucial one at that.

Help me to realize in the course of this day and tomorrow who I am and who You are, what I represent and what my witness is about. And take care of me. I love You.

February 14, 1991 — Somewhere over Ohio

My Love,

I'm an hour out of New York on the way to Dallas, still six hours from Tucson and the end of this seventeen-day interruption of my

Tucson interlude. I've put on weight, I have a cold or badly troubled sinus, I'm worn out. I can blame only myself, though I don't know that I would have cancelled anything — not the *Magic Flute*, not my birthday for sure, not this interlude in New York, which was a matter of simple justice for my publisher. I might have cancelled the Washington lecture, which was a flop, but then I did see Chris and Elizabeth and the lecture will appear as an article in *America*, and I couldn't have gone back for a week anyway. Besides, I like Chicago.

However, with Your help I will do so. Or at least do better.

I love You. I thank You for all the graces of this trip. I offer You the inconveniences and the troubles and I ask that You take care of me back in Tucson.

February 16, 1991 — Tucson

My Love,

Back in Tucson and utterly exhausted by the travel. Yesterday was a blur as I tried, foolishly I suppose, to catch up on everything. You did not mean for me to travel, of that I'm sure.

The poem I read this morning from the Midwest Collection quotes Walt Whitman that the man who has the sky and the air has everything. The plant, the tree, the cloud, the river — all these are enough for rejoicing. The metaphorical insight, the analogical imagination at work. I've been in three beautiful places during the last two weeks and noticed them only barely in passing. I must not only be renewed by the desert; I must also enjoy it during these weeks to come.

Both St. Paul and David in this morning's Scripture are railing against people, their right I guess and surely not the first or the last railers in our tradition: David against enemies and Paul against sinners. It's a natural enough response and one does not want to slip into an amorphous relativism in which there is no evil.

Yet I'm tired of railers, perhaps because there is so much of it in the pseudopatriotism of this foolish war. But, no, I've had too much railing during my life. Perhaps that is why I turn off the pope. He seems always to be moaning and complaining.

We need more positive stories of Your love and Your grace. I will try to make that especially true of the novel I'm writing—*The Allurements of Grace.*

February 17, 1991 — Tucson

My Love,

The cold weather has returned. I'm still very tired, very, very tired. I'm not depressed, just worn out. I suppose the depression will return if I'm not careful.

As I've said, I accept this tiredness, but I'd just as soon it would go away. So if You're a mind and can swing it, I'd be happy to recover some of my vigor — or more precisely to have the vigor last for more than morning and early afternoon.

I am, You should excuse the expression, tired of being tired.

I do love You and always will.

February 19, 1991 — Tucson

My Love,

I'm better today, perhaps because the sun is out, perhaps because I went to a movie last night (*Silence of the Lambs*, brr!), perhaps because I swam for half an hour. Help me to continue to get back my strength.

The news on Jack Durkin is not good. They will not operate this week but are sending him to see other specialists. Dear God, help him and help all the family. We all must die, yet we pray for life, begging You for a few more brief moments here on earth. You made us strange creatures, conscious of the brevity of our time, yet always wanting more till the physical pain of dying finally persuades us to give up.

Twenty thousand Iraqis dead, the news said this morning, and the ugly part of the war hasn't started yet. If the Bush administration wanted a way out, it could have one now, I think. But it doesn't want a way out. It wants total victory, no matter how many more Americans and Iraqis die. The evil is beyond contemplation.

There's nothing one can do—denounce it in columns, protest, not much more. The American people are as bent on total victory as Bush is, swept up by propaganda and by the ugliness of the enemy — we don't need propaganda to make Saddam appear evil. He's evil enough. But there seems so little compassion or concern for the civilians who have died, the little children who have been maimed. It is almost as though the country is *reveling* in war.

When our casualties come in, the tune will change. Yet I have to pray that there will be few American casualties because that means few will die on either side. Dear God, please, please let it end soon.

February 21, 1991 — Tucson

My Love,

Saddam Hussein this morning dashed all hopes of peace. The bloody ground war is now inevitable. Let it be quick and with as few casualties as possible. What terrible suffering, what terrible evil we do to one another! Does anyone need any more proof of human sinfulness?

This morning I read Psalm 147 as well as the Epistle to the Romans. The psalm celebrates the superiority of the Israelite people. St. Paul refutes that sense of superiority. Both works exist in a different context from our own and must not be judged or responded to in terms of our own insights, concerns, and problems. Paul is very difficult to understand and one is tempted to say that the issue of justification as he discusses it doesn't make much sense to us today — and that Luther's obsession with it was harmful to all concerned. Such a judgment of course throws out much of the Reformation/Trent debate as irrelevant today. I don't mind saying that, but I also think that Paul's warning about a sense of superiority, which really lies behind the text — or maybe *pace* Paul Ricoeur in front of it — is as valid today as it ever was. The war is being fought precisely because of two different cultures, both of which are convinced of their superiority.

In fact, worth and goodness, as Paul insists, comes from Your love — an answer to all jingoism, chauvinism, and hyperpatriotism.

It's a truth I surely believe, though I don't always act like I do. My only way of saying that on the subject of the war is to do so in my column. And that I shall do.

Again I conclude by begging for peace.

February 22, 1991 — Tucson

My Love,

There may be a chance for peace this morning. The struggle is over conditions, and at this point I agree with the president: Saddam cannot be permitted to end the war in a fashion which leaves him in a position to do the same thing all over again — this although I don't think the war was necessary. But I suspect he won't back down.

(I've put this reflection on hold for the last couple of hours and worked on something else while I listened to TV about the war. I don't mind working and listening, but it would seem kind of cheap to pray while keeping an eye and an ear on the tube.)

It seems to me that Bush's terms are so stark that Iraq will certainly reject them. It's the same old issue which has existed since last August: can we permit the enemy a little bit of face saving? Good negotiators should be able to do that. Obviously the American leadership is not prepared to and hence land war now seems inevitable — a high cost for refusing to hold out a bit of an olive branch to a defeated enemy.

I love You.

February 23, 1991 — Tucson

My Love,

The chances for peace have been up and down all morning. It doesn't look good at this minute. A Russian on TV is talking. Maybe they've pulled it off. Maybe not. How frail and limited we humans are when it comes to finding a way to get out of the messes we get ourselves into. It looks to me like the president wants a war and is quite unable to see that the other side is blinking like mad.

This has been a very crowded week. I've been catching up on work, trying to clear the desk before I turn to revising and writing novels. I'm feeling much better physically and have more energy, and hence am driving myself much too hard as I dispose of columns, correspondence, data analysis, and newsletter — as well as sustaining social relations out here and trying to lose weight.

The Russian didn't hold out much hope, but he's trying.

Please let there be peace and please help Jack Durkin in his search next week for health.

February 24, 1991 — Tucson

My Love,

The ground war has begun, so far so good. I pray for all those who have died and their families that You may wipe away their tears and their pain. Grant that it may end quickly.

Last night at the modern dance event over in Centennial Hall the question was raised as to why God has permitted so many people to die of AIDS. We continue to think that we are unique; we are the only ones to witness a holocaust or a fatal epidemic. We know nothing of history. The question might better have been asked of God at the time of the Black Death — or more recently the Spanish Flu.

The terrible thing is not that some die young, or some die in a holocaust, or that some die in a plague. The terrible thing is that anyone dies, that we all die eventually, that one person dies, even after eighty years of life. Why can't we see that death itself is the mystery and not numbers of deaths? Why do You permit us to be creatures with a hunger for immortality and consciousness of our own mortality? That is the question.

And there are not answers save that You suffer with us, You suffer with the Iraqi soldier who is awakened from his sleep to be torn apart by 20-mm cannon bullets.

Milosz says this morning that because of death he takes a little comfort from checkered skirts and pigtails. In the Twenty-third Psalm David describes death, a psalm which Jesus would later apply to himself.

There are no good ways of dying. We all die badly and, from our own perspective, much too soon.

Life is so bloody short and both those words are important. It is not fair that young men should die in this foolish war. It is not fair that widows and children should be left to mourn them. But the widows and children will die soon too.

And the mountains behind my house go on . . . as I must believe does Your love.

February 25, 1991 — Tucson

The war continues; it seems now that it will be quick and not too many more people on either side will be killed. Grant that it might be so.

St. Paul this morning in Romans 6 sounds the clarion call of Christian faith: through Jesus we triumph over sin and death. Yes, of course, isn't that the groundwork of our faith? The faith in resurrection of the Pharisees (of which Paul was one) reenforced by the Easter experience of the apostles?

Do I believe it? Verbally? I certainly do. In my head? Most of the time. In my whole soul and personality so that it transforms my life? To some extent, not as much as I should or would. Yes, death is not the end, I don't doubt that. But do I live free from worry and concern, from anxiety and fear, from compulsions and obsessions?

Not entirely, not by a long shot.

Today would be a good day to go back to serious prayer at morning and night and in between. It's a good day especially since I feel myself under constraints to clear up a lot of work today. It could easily be the sort of day which denies the resurrection — or one which affirms it.

Which will it be?

I love You. Help me to love You through this interesting test day. That's up to me, isn't it?

February 27, 1991 — Tucson

My Love,

The war is almost over. Saddam Hussein was a paper tiger after all. Thank God! (You, that is). Yet men and women have died. Grant them peace and joy. And heal the wounds of those who have suffered losses.

Rich Daley won the primary last night by more than two to one, no surprise. Nora and Patrick both looked great on TV.

I caught up on my sleep last night and am a little groggy this morning. I'm heading for the pool in a few minutes to try to clear the cobwebs out of my head.

Today I'm going to try again to interrupt progress periodically for prayer. Help me to remember.

This afternoon and evening I'm going to work on the revision of my mystery. So that should catch me up on everything.

I love You.

February 28, 1991 — Tucson

My Love,

The war is over! After four days! Thank You for the quickness and the victory. Grant that the violence in that part of the world is finished.

I'm at that part of the Epistle to the Romans where St. Paul talks about spirit and flesh and the struggle between the two, the good we want to do we don't do and the evil we don't want to do that we do — that original sin about which Martin Marty once said it is the only Christian doctrine for which there is empirical proof on the front page of the papers every day.

And one could add on CNN every hour of every day.

I rarely see any attention by contemporary theologians to the fact that much of our failure to do what we want to do or to avoid that which we want to avoid results from physical weakness, genetic predispositions, psychological propensities, sickness, weariness, frustration, and ignorance. How many of the mistakes I've made in my life were shaped in part by sinus headaches and lack of sleep and impatience with the clanging telephone. Or by the sense of being under constant attack, a sense that was not so silly as in my better moments in those days I thought it was.

I'm not making excuses. I'm sorry for what I did wrong. But I am rather trying to understand the nature of human weakness and striving to see what are its empirical manifestations. Sin in Paul's sense is ultimately our finitude and our fear. We don't do what we want to do because we are afraid and often because we are weary or sick or distracted.

Because we're creatures, and creatures aspiring to immortality.

Pretty battered and useless creatures a lot of the time.

But You still love us. And I try to love You in return.

March 1991

March 1, 1991 — Tucson

My Love,

Two metaphors in my Scripture reading this morning: You are a parent, not a master of slaves (St. Paul) and You are the sun (the psalmist). Not new metaphors surely. But powerful just the same. Especially the sun on this second "unsettled" (as they call it out here) day — clouds, rain, wind, cold. When the sun returns it will bring light, clarity, brightness, joy, especially to a light-sensitive creature like me.

Similarly when I perceive You as the source of my faith and the ground of my hope and the object of my love, life emerges from the darkness into the blinding light of the sun.

Right now I am in a dull, lethargic, somewhat troubled state. Most of it, as I said yesterday — or tried to say — is physiological. Some of it is spiritual. And my abiding spiritual problem of discouragement after overwork. I have worked hard these last two weeks and must work hard again today. I am discouraged, though not so weary as when the pneumonia was bugging me. Physical sunlight will clear away some of it. The rest will remain to be cleared away by spiritual sunlight, and I'll perceive that sunlight only when I find time for prayer in the course of a day.

I've known this all my life as a priest and I've never been able to do it really right for all my efforts. It's clear I never will do it without Your help for which on this cloudy day when we shall not see the sun I strongly beg.

I love You.

March 5, 1991 — Tucson

My Love,

I'm sorry that I've missed three days — a guest and an intestinal infection at the same time have kind of wiped me out. I'm feeling a little better this morning, but still not 100 percent — and the dinner in my honor is at El Charro tonight.

I accept this sickness as part of the human condition, but just the same I ask You to grant that I get over it as soon as possible.

I love You. I'll be back later.

March 8, 1991 — Tucson

This continues to be a hectic week. I'm over the stomach flu but still rushing with my guests. It's nice to have guests. Perhaps I overdo the role of host. On the other hand, by serving the guest I serve You, and that's what You want me to do.

Anyway I love You. Next week I'll be back in my regular routine for the last three weeks here.

March 10, 1991 — Tucson

My Love,

My guest goes home today. While it's nice to have visitors, it's also nice when they go home and I can settle back into my routine. I have three more weeks here before I return to Chicago. I don't feel much like working on a novel, so I'll do sociology and try to relax. It's been an odd winter, broken up by the interlude in Chicago, and slowed down by my recuperation from pneumonia, now complete, thank You.

Maybe I'm getting old, losing my ambition. I don't feel like working and so I'm not working! Or maybe it's the beginning of wisdom. Anyway, I'll be glad to get back to my reading and meditating tomorrow. I'm sorry if I've been sloppy in my prayers and reflections. I'm grateful for the time out here and for Your love. I'm grateful too for the guests and the love You send me.

March 11, 1991 — Tucson

My Love,

A gray Monday morning in Tucson and I'm busy catching up on the ideas generated during the last week of no work. I guess that is the story of my life — a brain that never stops working. It's a blessing for which I am grateful but also a demon which drives me all the time.

It's the way I am and I have no grounds for complaint.

I've turned to Irish poets, Thomas Kinsella and Philip Larkin, the latter at least of Irish origin. And I wonder this morning why poets are always sad. Both Kinsella and Larkin in the poems this morning lament the passage of life, its limitations and imperfections. Maybe poets are that way, maybe such a vision drives you to poetry, or maybe if you are a poet you see more clearly than others the limitations and imperfections of life. But it was interesting to read them in contrast to St. Paul's hymn that nothing can separate us from the love of God and David's poem about the courts of the Lord.

Something more, in other words, remains to be said after the sadness. I don't think that Kinsella or Larkin would deny that truth. They may be more reluctant than earlier poets to invoke the transcendent, and that may not be bad. One must not go beyond the tragedy of life too quickly to find the rumors of angels, but the rumors are still there.

That's what I want to write my own stories and poems about (if I ever get back to the poems) — the hints of the transcendent, the rumors of angels that point beyond tragedy, even, perhaps especially, in those poignant moments of joy and sadness when one knows that it will all end and yet senses that something more must be said — moments that abounded during the past week and on which I must reflect as this week goes on.

I love You, the One about whom the angels rumor.

March 12, 1991 — Tucson

My Love,

The poets continue this morning to agonize over what Kinsella calls the dread that lurks in love. Ovid again. Or was it Horace —

"O slowly, slowly run you steeds of night." In time of love mortality is especially threatening and especially conscious. We want at all times to be immortal but especially in times of intense love. Why must such love be doomed to end? Thus the central poignancy of the human condition.

In our dual article in the *New York Times* Rabbi Jacob Neusner said that the two of us believe in happy endings because we believe in the Resurrection of the Dead and the Life of the World to come, freedom for Israel from bondage and freedom for humanity from death.

I put that in the piece though I suspect that it will stir up lots of negative reaction, especially from Jewish readers. But indeed that is the answer to the dread that stalks love — the response that says that love is stronger than dread, strong as death itself, and yet stronger still.

I fear that we priests and perhaps we Catholics have used survival after death too easily as a weapon against dread. We have tried to deny or to repress dread and have hence lost our credibility with those who experience dread in its full terror.

We cannot tell people not to feel dread. Quite the contrary, we have to feel it with them and then reenforce their own instinctive sense that maybe, just maybe, love is stronger and that in the end love will conquer dread.

Of course we have to believe that ourselves. Our lack of belief may be the reason why we try to deny the power of dread. It won't work. It has to be faced in its fullness and then, like Michael Fox in the movie *Bright Lights, Big City*, faced down.

March 13, 1991 — Tucson

My Love,

In the poems this morning Larkin and Kinsella, as if plotting together to provide a common theme for me, continue to speak of dread and our efforts to avoid it by distancing ourselves from death, dying, and the dead. In his "Ambulances," Larkin notes how we pay so little attention to an ambulance racing through the streets or to the face of someone being lifted into the ambulance. Sure enough, though I always feel some compassion and a need to pray when an ambulance races by. Kinsella describes in

"Downstream" reflections on death during a night ride down a river because of a man who died on the bank—and how he tries, in vain, to distance himself from the feelings the man must have had as he died.

Both are correct in the sense that we know we are going to die but refuse most of the time to see ourselves in the position of the person dying. Larkin does not break out of the melancholy. Kinsella does at the sight of a bird taking off from the river and then the stars above. He encounters a "sacrament" if one wishes, though as he pulls ashore he realizes that he is only postponing dread and not overcoming it.

Fair enough.

And the psalmist this morning asserts that happy are the people who know how to rejoice in the Lord.

Amen.

My life, for all its rush, is based on that conviction. As I grow older I face dread more often and like Kinsella see the sacraments which counter it. Perhaps I don't face the dread honestly enough — though I intend when I'm back in Chicago to do some more things in preparation for death — and perhaps I don't reflect on the sacraments enough—though I intend to do that more often.

But I do know You love me and by that center of faith I live as long as You grant me life.

March 15, 1991 — Tucson

My Love,

A gift today for which I am thankful. It was supposed to be cloudy and rainy but in fact the sun is bright and the sky is clear even if it is cold. For that many, many thanks.

I'm not sure it's a good thing to keep reading these melancholy Irish poets. Both Larkin and Kinsella write today about the fragility of life and the inevitability of death—and today the psalmist joins in with the same theme.

Well, I'm not going to deny their point. On the contrary, I agree with it and I want to hear it more because I need it, we all need it. I can see it also as a theme to fit the next book.

But the other side must be said too. Perhaps Kinsella sees that too in "The Hen Woman." "There's plenty more where that came from." Life is prodigious, overwhelming. In that there is mystery, hint, and perhaps sacrament. The "perhaps" is his, not mine. The excessiveness of life is the best sacrament we could ask for, a hint of how powerful, how determined, and how excessive You are.

I believe that. Help me to believe it more.

March 19, 1991 — Tucson

St. Joseph's Day, the feast of the patron of a Happy Death, a festival ignored by the liturgists and loved by the people. Remember when Your servant Pope John put St. Joseph in the Canon of the Mass (Eucharistic Prayer now)? After he was dead the liturgists threw St. Joseph out!

The liturgists and the theologians have history, Scripture, and theology on their side. But St. Joseph has story on his side and hence will outlast all of them. The story tells more about You than do all the nonfiction articles and books: because of Your love as revealed through Jesus, death can be a happy event. Life, as the preface of the Requiem Mass says (I forget what it should be called now), is changed, not taken away. Surely Joseph knew that as he died. I believe we all get a chance to know that; some of us seize the chance; some don't.

One must die as befits a follower of Your son. Help me to do so when my time comes.

I pray this morning for all those who are dying or are in fear of death. Help us all to know how much You love us. And help me to remember what St. Joseph stands for.

March 22, 1991 — Tucson

My Love,

Both poets this morning, Larkin and Hutchinson, write about beaches — a nice image here in Tucson with its bitter cold (though You sent the sun, which was good of You under the circumstances) and myself coughing and sneezing. Both see the beach in summer as a kind of sacrament, a hint of what life means though both are reluctant to essay any guess as to what it does mean.

As I hardly need tell You, I'm a beach and summer freak. I see summer as a sacrament, too, though not as powerfully or perhaps I should say as articulately as our two poets. I believe in sacramentality and I can be more explicit about what lurks behind the metaphor, but I guess I don't pay enough attention to all the sacraments around me.

Hutchinson (Anglo-Irish, I'd wager) focuses on the scent of jasmine, as good a sacrament as one could imagine. How many times have I smelled it and thought of how lovely it was. Perhaps on occasion I even thought of it as a hint of what You are like, but I've never really paused to consider its full sacramental power.

I've managed to build up a frail habit of experiencing my keys as a reminder to prayer. How much further do I have to go to be open, not fully open, but a little more open to the sacramentality all around me?

You lurk everywhere — in my improving health against my cold, in the sunshine this morning, in the beaches, in my anticipation of Grand Beach, in the smell of the jasmine and of the creosote after a rainstorm, in the snow shining on the sunlight in the mountains.

How much richer my life would be and how much a better person and a better priest I would be if I could train myself to be sensitive to Your presence everywhere.

March 23, 1991 — Tucson

My Love,

I've started to read the memoir *Morning Light* of the French priest and novelist Jean Sulivan (a nom de plume from a Preston Sturgiss film!). He was an interesting, deep, and fascinating man. More haunted than I and perhaps more angry. Today he laments how much he bought the spirituality of his seminary — prosaic, cognitive, devoid of psychological insight. He admits that he did find out about Jesus there too, yet he found his real faith in the simple faith of his mother in the rural village where he was raised.

Faith is experiential before it is propositional, that's for sure. And often the propositions are more obstacle than help. But the faith experience must be very powerful for us Catholics because it has transcended so much inadequate articulation. I agree with Sulivan about the spirituality of the seminary. Perhaps because I am not as deep as he I found it easier to transcend. And I am not angry at the seminary teachers any more. They were a product of their time and place, of a different style of Catholicism than that in which we live today. They did a fairly good job, I guess, or I wouldn't be what I am today.

I do get angry at the phoniness and dishonesty of those who lead the Church today in this country. Unlike the seminary teachers, they know better — as I will say in my column for a week from Sunday.

Another phone call — not ten o'clock on Saturday morning and three phone calls! Gonna be a bad day!

I think I have the next novel figured out.

Anyway back to spirituality and the seminary. I've been very fortunate to be able to transcend those times and places, to have escaped and brought with me all that was good, often in rearticulated fashion, and to have put together a new, though as You well know, often pretty thin, spirituality.

Thank You for this opportunity. Help me to make the most of it.

March 24, 1991 — Tucson

Palm Sunday

Holy Week begins and my last week here. I'll be preparing to go home and trying to steep myself in the meaning of the Passover Triduum. It would be nice if there were a parish which was really mine so that I could sense I was celebrating the signal victory of life over death with a people. Well, that's not to be. I leave those issues to Your wisdom.

Today I am tired, or perhaps I should say sleepy, mostly pleasantly sleepy, a little bit discouraged sleepy. Feeling mortal, I guess, easily mortal. Wondering what all my effort and work during a busy and, some would think though perhaps not I, exciting life are worth. Jesus died and I will die. He rose and I will rise — because of Your Love. That I believe.

What does anything else matter? Why do I try so hard? Why

do I fight so bravely? Why this integrity which forces me to the margins? So what?

"It all seems to me as dust," Aquinas wrote. So I feel on Palm Sunday—with more of a reason than Aquinas, but still without a good reason. I have tried to do what I think You wanted me to do. Dust, but dust sanctified by You, and by Jesus, and by promise.

I labor, however inadequately and incompletely, for the Promise. Help me always to do so as long as You give me life.

March 25, 1991 — Tucson

My Love,

I continue to read Jean Sulivan. He rails against the institution this morning with considerable vigor—it thinks it has a monopoly on the Word but is not open to conversion by it! Nicely put!

He suggests that a break from the institution is something that is not only regrettable but necessary, and in fact a positive good. Now that's a thought I have to ponder. I have always tended to think that my alienation from the archdiocese is an unfortunate accident caused by peculiarities of time and place and people. It was certainly not something I wanted or sought like Sulivan apparently did. It happened. It bestowed a certain freedom at the price of a certain alienation. It was part of Your plan. I would make the most of the marginality given me.

But here's where I think I have been different from Sulivan and perhaps incorrect. If ever the chance came to return to the institution on my own terms and with no loss of freedom, I would do so. He tells me that freedom from the institution is a positive good, and that it should never be given up.

I suspect that, granted a certain Gallic exaggeration, he is right. Even the hope of being accepted again by one's colleagues and bishop is deceptive. It deprives me somewhat of my freedom and it suggests that I might be waiting for a day of vindication. Not wise, not wise at all. It would never be more or less on my own terms. I would have to compromise. And, having been given my freedom by You as a pure grace, I should not think of compromise and must exorcise from myself all thought of a willingness to compromise.

Seems reasonable all right. I'll have to reflect on it.

March 26, 1991 — Tucson

My Love,

"I humiliated the Word," Sulivan says in the passage today, in the name of ideologies and sentiments. So he left the active ministry to become a writer so that he "would lie less."

Fierce Gallic logic! Did I ever humiliate the Word? Maybe in the birth control business in the 1950s and 1960s — from ordination to the time I read John Noonan's book, I was enforcing a rule I learned in the seminary, without much sympathy or compassion. I guess a lot of us priests learned from that terrible experience to distrust the institutional leadership and what it tried to do to the people. Still other priests are using other excuses to control the lives of the laity — sometimes in the name of liberal principles at that.

Well, I've perhaps made up for that, although the institution with its sex obsession has not.

I guess one does not have to go quite as far as Sulivan to realize how skeptical one must be about the institution, recognizing that a heritage needs an institution and the institution needs some loyalty and has the right to some loyalty, but within limits. Certainly not institution worship. Birth control and John Cardinal Cody — those twin experiences cured me of institutional worship. However, the cure put me on the outside of the institution in many ways. Okay, that's a good thing, though it would perhaps be better if the institution were open enough to value strong criticism from within. It isn't now and it can't be because it is so afraid.

Well, the twelve apostles weren't much either.

"For the good of the Church" on the lips of a priest or a bishop normally means for the good of the power elite who control the Church and certainly not for the good of the people.

Who cares about the people?

Well, You have given me a direct link to the people through my books and I must be careful to sustain that link and keep it authentic and ignore what the institutional critics say.

Help me to steer the delicate middle course that this venture requires.

March 29, 1991 — Tucson

My Love,

Thus far I'm spending Good Friday morning trying to get organized to go home on Monday, activity which is more manic than usual because I'm revising two papers and dismantling my computer set-up here. By noon it should all be finished and I can relax, pray a little, and maybe write Holy Week poetry. I sure hope so.

Last night I preached about the Eucharist as a delicious dessert, a fair enough historical as well as symbolic observation, and the priest as the one who sees that the dessert is served. We are responsible for the sweetness of life. Moreover, so too are all followers of Jesus supposed to bring sweetness to those they love.

It was fun. I asked the other priests (with warning) what their favorite dessert was: rhubarb pie, without ice cream, for the monsignor, and a number of kids chose pumpkin pie.

I hope I can remember Your sweetness whenever I eat dessert, especially chocolate dessert.

I do Love You. I'm grateful for the idea of dessert and for the idea of the Easter bunny on Sunday.

March 30, 1991 — Tucson

My Love,

This Holy Saturday morning Sulivan rails against theology — "weak soup for the dead," he calls it, abstractions which have replaced faith. The Good Friday experience last night resonates nicely with such a critique. On the level of ritual and symbol it is wonderful (even if I was too sleepy), but the theology of redemption — Jesus paying a price to persuade God to forgive us (which the young priest used in his sermon, a very moving sermon nonetheless) — is offensive. I suspect most people ignore the theology though it still kind of floats around as background noise.

Where I'd differ with Sulivan is that I think we need good theology to help us articulate what the imagery and rituals mean. The "blood price theology" exists because there's nothing better to exorcise it. Theologians are hard put to do that because of fear of the Vatican and because they are caught in the paradigms of past theological reflection.

Anyway, I take it that Your son died to show us how to die and to show that love or Love risks itself even unto death. This makes great good sense and for the moment that's all I need — at least on the level of theory.

No, I would add: Jesus died to show us how *Love* risks death with the conviction that *death is not the end.* Love rises from the dead. We don't know how that happens — and much of the argument among theologians about resurrection is foolish for that reason — but we do know that it happens.

My death cannot be far into the future as time goes. I must identify with Jesus so that however I die, I will die bravely as he did and with the conviction that Love is stronger than death.

I think that's what Good Friday means.

March 31, 1991 — Feast of the Lord's Resurrection

My Love,

Tomorrow I leave here with the same ambivalences with which I leave every year — sad to depart Tucson, glad to return to Chicago. The ambivalences will never go away, but that's all right. The life here is a blessing for which I will always be grateful.

This feast of Your son's resurrection makes us believe in happy endings — and beginnings — as I told the people in my sermon at Our Mother of Sorrows this morning. I lament the shallowness of my life and of my spirituality. And I hope with Your help to make it deeper in the days and weeks ahead. The key is working at it. Maybe I'll try to write a religious poem every week. No, that's too many. How about one a month, beginning tomorrow, April 1? Maybe that will help me acquire a little more spiritual depth.

I also understand that such depth is a gift and You love me without it. My challenge is not to stand in Your way.

April 1991

April 1, 1991 — Tucson

My Love,

I'm on the Tucson-to-Chicago plane about to take off. Already the clock reads CST instead of MST. Back to the Middle West, back home. Can't beat that! I face the end of winter and the beginning of spring, not exhausted but renewed and refreshed. There'll be the transitional strain of course, but I'm going to try to diminish that. And, as always, I've managed to schedule another flight before the week is over. So by next weekend I'm likely to have lost a little of my good spirits. But not, I think, too much.

Anyway, thank You very much for the Tucson time. Help me to adjust smoothly to Chicago. Help me to continue to link keys with prayer and to begin my resolution to write a poem every month.

April 5, 1991 — Hartford, Connecticut

My Love,

I'm at Bradley Field ready to fly home from Hartford. I am so sorry about the last three days, either rushing like mad to get organized or, as yesterday, not being able to figure how this new computer works on batteries. However, I'll soon be home and the transition will be over and I can settle down to what I hope is a reasonable routine.

There's no real excuse for Tuesday and Wednesday. I had a lot to do, but I could have, should have, taken off a few minutes for prayer. Forgive me — though in truth I didn't have much time to call my human loves either, which was also an exercise in selfishness.

I'm afraid I'll have to go on "Nightline" tonight to comment on this crazy exorcism program that was televised. A disgrace to the Church. I must not lose my temper.

The reviews of my novel in the newspapers this morning were all very favorable. It's so nice when thoughtful people read my fiction and like it and understand it. That gives me a new push to go on, not that I needed the push, I suppose. I do go on. But sometimes the criticism makes me feel that I'm not a good writer. On a morning like this I know that I am and for that I am very grateful indeed.

Now no more trips till I leave for Ireland a month from now!

I love You, and I know that You love me even when I forget about our love.

April 7, 1991 — Chicago

My Love,

First day of daylight saving time, how I welcome that sacrament of spring and of You, the Eternal Daylight.

Sulivan is very good this morning on the danger of turning the Word, Your Word, into an ideology, an official, univocal version of the Gospel. The fundamentalists do it, poor people, but we do it too with our institution and pope worship. "The Word is to be found in story," he says. He gives a deeper and richer meaning to story than I had thought of before — and to my own work in stories, which I do not value enough.

I must run now to Leo Mahon's fortieth anniversary Mass. Bless him and protect him. He is one of the truly good priests.

April 9, 1991 — Chicago

My Love,

Leo's anniversary was very moving. A certain bishop made a fool out of himself by a mean-spirited commentary after Mass, which was just the opposite of what Leo has stood for — ideology replacing generosity, in Jean Sulivan's words. Why is there so little generosity in the Church? So little willingness to leave room for others? So much need to restrict, to limit, to draw boundaries, to exclude? Leo has been generous all his life and is an outcast, though not as much as I am, because of that.

Yet that is the only way to go. A one-message reading of the Gospel is ideology and power, a destruction of the Word. I must make that theme clearer in my novels — if I ever get down to writing them again.

And I must try to practice it in my own life and to respect and value the opportunity for generosity that my own freedom provides. I'm in a bad mood this morning. Help me to get over it or at least keep it under control. I love You.

April 11, 1991 — Chicago

My Love,

I have been working on my book of prayers the last two days and I offer them as my reflections at least for yesterday. I hope You don't think that's cheating. No, I mean I hope You don't mind that cheating!

We're celebrating my thirty-seventh anniversary in the priesthood tonight since I'll be in Ireland on May 5. Time to reflect on all those years.

I pray today for all my classmates and for all those who are celebrating anniversaries — Bill Quinn at fifty, Leo Mahon at forty, Bob McLaughlin at twenty-five. Grant that there be more priests and better priests like them to do Your work for You in the world.

April 12, 1991 — Chicago

My Love,

We had a wonderful anniversary party last night, really wonderful, for which I am deeply grateful. I told my dessert story, which was well received and which is an excellent object lesson for me as to what a priest should be — the one who provides the dessert, the one who brings out the sweetness in life.

But I am tired again this morning as I always am after one of those events, tired and discouraged about my inability to pull away from everything else and write a single word of the novel. So much else demands my time and energy and the novel is, like I say, how I earn my living. I had hoped to get to it today, but it doesn't look like that will happen either.

Forgive me for being so distracted. I do love You. My human weaknesses are especially obvious to me today. I'm hardly the dessert-maker that I know a priest should be.

April 15, 1991 — Grand Beach

My Love,

I'm back in the delight and the agony of storytelling. I worked until about eight last night, which was a mistake because the story haunted me for several more hours. I should never, repeat never, write fiction after supper.

It's a good story and it's coming along fine. I thank You for the storytelling talent of which for most of my life I was unaware. I thank You too for the hundreds of letters I receive, letters from ordinary people who reassure me when some priests and some reviewers make me feel doubt about my vocation as a novelist.

It's cold and rainy again, and there's a fierce wind. And I'm driving into the city for a Cubs' night game this evening. It's like writing after supper; I should know better! Anyway it will be fun!

Also once again I make up my mind to head for the Black Hills sometime this spring. Why do I say that? Because a night game and the Black Hills are like the same thing — something to do just because You haven't done it before!

I love You. It has been, despite the rain and the cold, a good weekend of rest. I'll be looking forward to coming back for a week in May after the Ireland trip. Let me thank You once again for the important part this place has played in my life.

April 16, 1991 — Chicago

My Love,

Well, I went to my first baseball game in forty years last night and my first major league night game ever. And, do You know what, I loved it! Mind You, I won't be in any rush to do it again, but it was fun. For which many thanks.

Jean Sulivan continues to plug away at his theme of the use of simplistic theological categories to achieve power over other human beings. Dear God, how much we have done that in ages past, ages hell, in *years* past.

I didn't do all that much of it in my years at Christ the King because You had blessed me early with skepticism about ideology, but I did some of it, particularly on birth control, for which I am now both ashamed and sorry.

If anything, the danger can be in the opposite direction today, a time when many priests don't seem to believe in anything at all. But that is the price we have to pay for the ideological constraints and rigidities of the past.

Anyway, I want to put some of that in my new novel, not to use it to preach (I couldn't get away with that) but structure it into the story, make the world a more problematic place in which grace works its miracles (*Your* miracles) in strange ways.

I'm going to try to build up again my habit of praying during the day, a habit which was doing pretty well in Tucson but did not survive the transition.

I love You. Now to the pool.

April 19, 1991 — Chicago

My Love,

A wonderful surprise.

The assistant dean at the University of Chicago called me this morning to tell me that I was being offered a five-year visiting professorship in the social sciences at the College.

I admit that I do feel elated. It's been a twenty-two-year battle, two years of discussion this time around. It's nice to win, nice to come home. Better late than never.

Validation as a sociologist? Not, I think, in the profession which knows my work, but in the world beyond the profession and in the priesthood it will be something of a validation, though those that don't like me will continue not to like me.

I will, however, celebrate in the days and weeks ahead and I also express now "on the record" the gratitude I expressed to You yesterday when I first received a hint of the news. Thank You for this victory. It is not essential, but it is still nice and I am very grateful indeed.

I'm sufficiently Irish to think that maybe there'll be a price to be paid. But You don't work that way. Of course there is a price as in every change, but that goes with the territory. No extra price merely because you won a victory.

I resolve never to claim any more than what has been won. I will be a "visiting professor" in all my credits. It will be very nice to "visit" Chicago! A great place to visit and a great place to live!

Anyway, I'm happy — and again very, very grateful.

It would be nice if the Church would go and do likewise, but that will never happen.

I love You.

April 21, 1991 — Chicago

My Love,

Sorry about yesterday. I knew when I started playing with the sociological data on prayer that it would be hard to get back to this reflection, especially since I was going through the agony of trying to clean the apartment at the same time as I was doing the data analyses.

I've been really pushed these last three weeks, especially this week. The demands of phone and mail and social life are notably impeding my ability to write the new novel. Indeed there is an order for some stuff on my desk which has sat there for a solid week because I had not had time to sit down and write it out, a few minutes work. I hope it's better this week. At least there's only one supper — at the end of the week, so I can go to bed early and get up at 5:00 and get my three thousand words a day (a modest enough expectation I should think) done before the phone starts ringing.

I'm complaining again, for which I'm sorry.

I'm grateful that in the rush I'm still able to pray during the day, a notable improvement over other rushed times.

Help me to keep that up, please.

I love You. Sorry for the rush.

April 23, 1991 — Chicago

My Love,

I've been up since 5:00 A.M. and it will be fifteen more minutes before I get to the novel — three hours of early morning productive time consumed with distractions (like beginning to pack for Ireland). I must resolve to go immediately to the pool, postpone the papers till later in the day since they are less subject to distractions, and do my spiritual reading the night before. Thus I can begin at six and have three hours instead of beginning at eight and have one hour. The only way I can write fiction is to keep those hours from 6:00 to 9:00 A.M. sacred.

Sorry to bother You with all the details and struggles of my life. However, it helps to know that You listen and You care even about such trivial matters as scheduling my day.

I also must stop working by suppertime, like I didn't do last night, if I expect a reasonably good night's sleep.

Tomorrow I will be finished with my three thousand words by 9:00 A.M. and take my video camera and head for the Morton Arboretum to welcome Your spring.

Having gone through all this scheduling hassle, I must now reflect on Seamus Heaney's beautiful poetry about respecting the world in which we live, and Jean Sulivan's raging against the hypocrites in the Church. I'll leave Sulivan till tomorrow — I think I finally begin to understand him and see the importance of institutional constraints, which he does not see and perhaps should not be expected to see.

I charge into reality instead of reveling in it. Watch, tomorrow I'll charge into the arboretum, trying to "do" the whole thing instead of savoring at some length bits and pieces of it (I hope this is a false prediction!). Remember the time I flew to Sedona and returned on an early plane? I had *done* Oak Creek Canyon!

I know You love me no matter what I do, but You must be fed up with this attack on life, indeed as it is displayed in the first half of this reflection.

Help me to slow down and enjoy!

I realize that's a big order and that all I can ever expect, given who and what I am, is some improvement and that with lots of Your help.

I love You.

April 25, 1991 — Chicago

My Love,

The arboretum yesterday was wonderful, meadows crowded with daffodils and daisies, flowering trees and the native forest with its wildflowers and fallen trees and lacy emerging greenery. All very spectacular on a warmish spring day.

April is indeed the cruelest month of the year — nature striving painfully to be reborn. But, despite the pain, it rebirths. I wonder as I try to absorb so much beauty — and then return here to appreciate it again on the miracle of videotape — if there be so much beauty on one tiny planet in a small solar system in an unimportant galaxy in (as far as we know) an ordinary cosmos, how much other beauty may lurk in Your creation, how much even in this world which we cannot see because our vision is limited to a narrow segment of the electromagnetic spectrum?

I ask myself, why did You bother? We dare not have the arrogance to believe that this beauty is limited to our planet, that there is no one else to see it. But with so much in creation, why did You bother to make this blue planet so beautiful? Why was it worth the effort? This blue planet is insignificant, seemingly unimportant, yet You have made it painfully beautiful. Why?

The answer, I think, is that is the way You do everything. Beauty — mighty and small — delights You. This tiny planet delights You. This is a place made sacred by the coming of Your son — even if there are many other planets to which he has come.

I'm dazzled, overwhelmed, humbled — and above all grateful.

April 26, 1991 — Chicago

My Love,

Let's reflect on life and death this morning — not exactly a new subject. Seamus Heaney's poems deal with funerals and death, both in modern Ireland and in the bogs from which bodies are removed, a phenomenon which fascinates him, perhaps because the ritual killings remind him of the ritual murders in Ulster today.

They're astonishing poems. He's well on his way to becoming the best poetic voice in the English language in this century.

I think about death as the flowers in my apartment wither and as I reflect that the daffodils and daisies out at the arboretum will not last much longer either. I wonder why You permit such loveliness to have such a short life. Perhaps because I wonder why human loveliness has to wither and die so soon.

Then I read Sulivan about Jesus and surprise.

If I believe in anything at all, I believe in surprise. So the young woman in the bog whom Heaney mourns will rise again, perhaps to congratulate him and thank him for celebrating her. So will the relatives he buried, and those killed in the violence in Northern Ireland. And in Iraq. And the flowers. And all of us. We will all be young again.

I do believe that. I don't know how it will all happen. But I know it *will* happen because I believe in Your Love and that You are the God of wonder and surprise.

I love You. Thank You.

April 27, 1991 — Chicago

My Love,

April grinds to a close. Only a few more days and I leave for Ireland. It has been a hectic month as I try to adjust to living in Chicago, get ready for the trip, catch up on all my local responsibilities, and prepare for both the trip and the summertime. I get home on Monday night, as You know, and have something to do every night that week. I'll be a basket case. It would be much better for me to leave promptly for Grand Beach, but there are obligations which make that impossible.

How can it be, *pace* Sulivan this morning, that we have so missed the point of the parables, the proverbs, and the person of Jesus, a message of intimacy with You? How have we turned it into rules, doctrines, power structures, and fear? The perversion of Christianity is the worst of all perversions because it perverts the most hopeful and most loving of all religious traditions. There is perhaps no more obvious evidence of the existence of original sin in the world. It must anger the hell out of You, if You will excuse the expression. I'm going to preach on that this afternoon at St. Mary of the Woods.

I also must practice what I preach. I try in these reflections to do so, to treat You like an interested lover. In some sense that is blasphemy. How can as paltry a creature as I am pretend to such an intimacy? The answer is that I don't pretend to it. I respond to an intimacy that is offered to me — for reasons that escape me, as I guess all real love escapes explanation.

I believe this metaphor, I believe it with all my mind, and, as best I can, with all my heart too. Help me to grow in my belief and in my affection and in my life.

April 29, 1991 — Chicago

My Love,

This morning Sulivan describes the nature of Christianity perfectly — it is the hand of Jesus on your shoulder in friendship and threat, a fraternal and dangerous invitation.

Both aspects of the invitation are important. Neither can be diminished without missing the point completely. Jesus is a threat, a strange, disconcerting, sometimes terrifying person. But he also is a close friend, a brother, someone who will always be with you on the road.

If anything, I think the friendship is more often ignored than the threat. People were taught when I was growing up to fear You and Jesus with rather little mention given to the friendship and love dimension. Yet when one shifts over as I have done to the latter, it is so easy to domesticate Jesus (and You), to brush away the mystery, the wonder, the surprise, the *tremendens* of Rudolph Otto, the terror of an encounter with the Other.

The danger in my life most often is that I'm not disconcerted enough. Well, sometimes. The other danger is that I don't feel the friendly reassuring hand often enough. I guess I tend to swing from either end of this delicate balance.

I also lack confidence in my own reading of You for others. Or do I? Was I too nondirective with the old group at Grand Beach? Did I give up too easily?

It's a long time since I asked that question. I don't think I gave up too quickly. Rather perhaps not quickly enough, but I was certainly unsure in my ministry to them.

Maybe being unsure is what I should be. Yet Sulivan, rightly I think, stresses the confidence of Jesus in Mark's Gospel, the decisiveness of his actions. I'm afraid that I have often not been decisive enough.

And now my main concern so much of the time is fighting off the distractions to my work. It gets in the way of any kind of decisive and confident sense that I have been in touch with Mystery and know which way It's going.

An unresolved and unresolvable question. Nonetheless I must be more open toward and respectful of Mystery.

April 30, 1991 — Chicago

My Love,

I've been home now from Tucson for a month and am still running hard. It's been a very difficult time. It looks like it will continue to be difficult when I come back for most of May and maybe June too. I'm fed up with the pace and demands of life. I'll have to change, I just will have to change.

Breakfast, lunch, and supper yesterday! Ugh! I'm bloated.

Today I dread the trip to Ireland. I've taken on responsibilities for both other people's fun and for the meeting. I'll be running around like crazy and I'll be doing the same thing when I come back.

Why do I get myself into these messes!

As You can tell, I'm in a grim mood this morning, grim, grim, grim. Maybe I should have gone swimming first. Why so melancholy? The weather? The news of death and destruction on the radio, this time because of floods and storms and earthquakes, a general sense of the melancholy nature of human existence?

I don't know why, but I feel down this morning, even though I believe in Your love for me.

Maybe I'm just getting old.

Help me to cheer up, please.

If I dare ask for such a favor.

May 1991

May 1, 1991 — Chicago

The first of May, Mary's month, the month of the Galilean peasant girl who for two thousand years has been the sacrament of Your mother love for all of us. Help me during this chaotic, busy month never to forget that You do love us as a mother.

I drove out to the seminary yesterday for the Meyer lecture series. It was the first time I have been there in twelve years anyway and maybe longer. I was well received. Maybe [journalist] Tim Unsworth is right that lots of priests now know and respect my work. Anyway, the lecture was good and the seminary seems in good physical condition. Even a friend who teaches at the seminary admits, however, that the quality of seminarians isn't what it used to be. That fact bodes ill for the future of the Church.

Moreover, the vocation shortage, like all the other problems in the Church, is not destined, is not the result of fate; it rather has been caused by miserably bad leadership. Unlike "Sulivan" I cannot dismiss the institution as useless despite its power hunger, its ideology, its folly. One must have the Church; it is a sacrament. I would add, a sociologically necessary sacrament.

But right now it is mired in an irrelevance which is matched only by its arrogance. I'm glad I'm not part of it, but I'm sorry that it has rejected the talents I could have brought to its service.

Well, that's all too late and I'm not going to fight Your plans for me.

The official letter from the university came through yesterday.

A battle of twenty-two years is finally resolved. Strange, it seems now to make so little difference to me.

Quid hoc ad aeternitatem, as we used to say in the mother language.

Take care of me and the little group for which I have assumed responsibility in this Irish adventure.

And, if it be Your will, let us have some nice weather.

May 5, 1991 — Dublin

My Love,

Sunday morning in Dublin, gray and cloudy, but it has been reasonably nice, for which many thanks.

I'm waiting for the hotel pool to clear out. My friends are going up to New Grange. Our meeting starts this afternoon. So far they've had a good trip and are getting to know and like (very much) Ireland. I am struggling with the usual depression which comes from jet lag and travel. I feel worn out, old, frustrated. I don't display these emotions, which are physiological rather than mental, and will pass, more or less, when I go home.

Right now I hang on and trust in You and ignore the intermittent feeling that I have wasted my life, which I know isn't true — though it would be right to say that I haven't learned yet how to love You enough, but I'm still trying.

Help me through this venture and through the rest of my life, no matter how short or long it might be.

I love You.

May 8, 1991 — Dublin

I'm in the Dublin airport waiting for the plane to Galway, where I will rejoin my friends to have a drink tonight with Eammon Casey, bishop of Galway, and celebrate Steve and Susan's twentieth wedding anniversary. The meeting is over and my head is whirling with sociological questions, for which I unfortunately — and stupidly — brought the wrong data files.

The meeting went well and my friends have had a great time, for all of which many thanks.

Right now I'm just barely holding together and, as I always am, when a trip is half over, I am eager to get home.

But good has been accomplished, and for that I'm grateful.

I love You. Help me through the rest of this trip.

May 9, 1991 — Galway City

My Love,

Not a bad day, at all, at all, though too rainy this morning to make the trip to the Aran Islands — as at every other time I've been here! My guests are thoroughly taken in by Ireland and love it. So I have contributed my share of Irish hospitality to them — it's catching if you have the genes in you!

We met Eammon this afternoon and he took us around to the cathedral, the chapel at the university, and one of his new churches, and he entertained us all spectacularly. He deeply impressed everyone, God bless him. What a wonderful priest!

And what a wonderful country with such a terrible history! Grant rest to all the poor innocent people who suffered and died here, often terrible deaths, and grant that those of us who survive may always be grateful for the blessings of our freedom and prosperity.

Continue to bless us and protect us on this trip, please, and bring us home safely.

I love You and I thank You for all the good times.

May 17, 1991 — Chicago

Back home and with so much to do that I'm bumbling around trying to figure out where to start. It's now a month and a half since I came home from Tucson and I have not for a minute stopped running. Apart from the week which starts Sunday evening at Grand Beach I will continue to run for the next six weeks. This is absurd, crazy, sick. It's not my doing in the sense that it is my own work, none of this crazy weekend is that. The whole time will be consumed with social obligations to others which I cannot neglect. The week at Grand Beach will be a respite but then it will be back again. Please help me to escape this rat race before it kills me. Quite literally.

The performance of my play last night was a disaster. For forty minutes three hundred generous people sat in the chapel at Quigley Seminary in the steaming heat and heard not a single word of what was being said because the theater company did not use the microphones which Quigley offered them. I wished the ground would open up and swallow me. I was responsible for the mess because I let them use my name and my play as part of their fundraising. I didn't want to do it and ought to have known better, so I guess I deserved the humiliation. Never again.

I'm off to St. Louis University for an honorary doctorate this afternoon. I'm worn out. Help me, please!

And, I must add, I'm sorry for all the self-pity in this cry for help.

May 18, 1991 — St. Louis University

I'm here today to collect an honorary doctorate, which is nice. Also nice is that by being away from Chicago I am away temporarily from the rush. However, I'll be back to it this afternoon.

This gray, humid morning brings me a powerful sense of the tragedy of life. A good friend has lost his bank because one of the directors apparently absconded with a couple of million dollars. I also saw a grammar school classmate and his wife at dinner last night. He is retired early as president of his company because of a bad back. His wife endured eleven pregnancies to produce five children, one of whom, a little girl, died of cancer at the age of nine. At breakfast this morning I met some of my old Jesuit friends, all of whom have aged and some of whom are depressed.

Life is no picnic.

I also learn that Ted Mackin, the great Jesuit theologian of marriage, has at the age of sixty-nine left the priesthood and married. I wonder if his work ever received enough credit from his own.

I tell myself how fortunate I have been in comparison. My troubles are minor. I have no cause for complaint or self-pity — and no reason to think that there won't be more troubles in my life.

But, on the other hand, I must admire the way my friends deal with their problems, and the happiness my classmate and his wife have with their children and grandchildren and their admiration for my niece Annie Durkin. And I wonder if I have enough faith and enough maturity to cope with such assaults or with the inevitable advance of age. And I pray to You to help and sustain me in my confidence in Your love.

I'm on a high these days, as I usually am, when I come back from a trip — filled with insights and ideas — and also as usual I don't have nearly enough time to do anything about them. I am dispensing myself at the moment from two sociology projects and granting myself September as another month of vacation, not planning to start the next Blackie book till October. I hope I can take this "dispensation" seriously.

I love You.

May 19, 1991 — Chicago

My Love,

The rushing continues. Tonight at Grand Beach it will stop at least for awhile. I'm off for a Mass and two parties and then it will be over at least for a time, thanks be to You!

A party of celebration at the Colemans last night, double celebration because Jim's tests are proving good and he may be cured of the cancer, though that was a secret.

It was a very good and generous party, a celebration of loyal friends in a big victory. Yet I was so tired from the traveling and from the rushing that it swept by without my being able to savor it the way I ought to have.

I hope to simmer down at the lake. I'll be working a lot, up at five, write five thousand words before ten, then turn to sociology and articles, and then hopefully have time to revise and relax in the evening.

At least that's the design. Grant that I may be able to carry it out along with a good swim every day and a slowing down of the organism before I destroy it altogether.

Help me to bank down the fires just a little bit.

And thank You for the victory party last night.

I love You.

May 20, 1991 — Grand Beach

My Love,

I just about collapsed last night when I finally got here to Grand Beach. I'm really tired. I've decided to postpone all obligations till I am refreshed and reinvigorated. I don't think I've ever been so tired in all my life, except when I was recovering from pneumonia. I'll be back later.

I love You.

May 21, 1991 — Grand Beach

My Love,

I am beginning to feel better, though not yet ready to start the novel. It's astonishing how much difference it makes to be immune from the rushing in Chicago. Even the constant telephone calls don't bother me as much as they did there. Thank You for giving me a place like Grand Beach at which to relax.

Last week I went out to Altgeld Gardens [a housing project] and Robbins with Barry to visit Mary Kay. At both places I must say that the spirit of Vincent DePaul was still alive, nuns, a Vincentian brother, lay people, working with the poorest of the poor in impoverished, depressing, and often dangerous environments. I admire them enormously and feel how inferior my own work is in comparison with theirs.

I don't mean that I should stop my work and rush out there, though life would be much simpler if I did that. I'm doing what Your spirit wants me to do. I mean rather that I should keep in mind their example and not let the problems and difficulties and frustrations of my work seem too enormous or disturbing. There's no grounds for self-pity in my life, especially when I consider my being here at Grand Beach while they continue to work in the most challenging situation.

My mission is a valid one. It's what You want me to do. But it is not the most admirable of vocations. *Theirs is,* of that there can be no doubt.

I was terribly proud of my former teenagers now working in the suburban slums. Take care of them and help them and keep their faith and their hope high.

May 22, 1991 — Grand Beach

My Love,

This is the best time of the year at Grand Beach, the time when one is getting ready for summer and its prospects stretch out limitlessly. This summer will be busier than others, with the book promotion tours at the beginning and the visitors from Ireland at the end, but it will still be a good summer, because whether a summer is good or not is within my capacity to create — with Your help I hasten, almost with Irish superstition, to add.

This will be a serene summer. I have only a small number left and must treasure each one of them as the great blessing You have made it for me.

My different lifestyle from those brave people on whom I reflected yesterday is justified especially if I use it to improve my own ministry. That requires that I relax during the summer.

Please help me to do so.

Aging struck me again at the Coleman party and Erica's party the next day. I didn't recognize some of the guests because they were so changed since the last time I saw them, many fifteen years ago. I've undoubtedly changed too. We all grow older, life is short, its moments must be treasured.

But if I'm to believe Tom Harpur (and I do), as we grow older we become or can become more light, preparing for the Light that is to come. I love You. Help me this summer.

May 24, 1991 — Grand Beach

My Love,

The signs of Memorial Day abound — more traffic on the road, though it's still Friday morning, flowers for sale everywhere, green grass, blossoming trees, people on the streets of New Buffalo, an occasional hint of sunshine in the sky.

Very occasional, since You decided to tolerate this horrible week of rain which has soaked everything and produced swarms of mosquitos (their purpose baffles me as much as it did St. Augustine) all around and it's still May!

Anyway summer opens officially this evening. I look forward eagerly to another wonderful summer in my life, for which many,

many thanks. Summertime is a perfect metaphor for Your warmth and love. It is a guarantee, suited to our small and seemingly insignificant planet, of the warmth and love which beats at the heart of the universe.

You.

If my summers here on earth are now severely limited, I know that an eternal summertime with You stretches out ahead of me. Just now no other alternative seems possible. Help me to enjoy this summer as a hint of what is to come. Help me to believe that more strongly.

And also to believe, as in the fairy tale I saw on video the other night, that the Winter Queen really reflects You too.

(Also please stop the rain if You can.)

Thank You for everything. May You have a glorious weekend, celebrating along with all Your children.

May 26, 1991 — Grand Beach

My Love,

I am kind of depressed today, nothing special except, as You well know, a week of solid rain does that to me. Also I'm not eager for the minor facial surgery which I must undergo on Wednesday. That is par for the course if you are human, but I do ask You to take care of me.

I say only half-jokingly when I consider the surgery on Monday, squeezed in with five other obligations, that when the time comes for me to die, I will not have time to fit it into my schedule.

That's one way to avoid it. But also no way to live.

I look at next week's schedule and note that almost all of it is for other people as are most phone calls. It's difficult to say no, especially because I'm a priest and priests don't say no. But how I often dread the ring of the phone or the doorbell — even up here people are constantly at the door — and the sight of a crowded weekly calendar.

Well, it's part of the human condition and maybe part of my chosen purgatory, and I should not complain, given all the other blessings in my life. When I do complain it is because I understand that You are a lover and like all lovers willing and eager to know how I feel.

Will I stay on my schedule next week for novel writing?

Why not? There are only two nights that I won't be able to get to bed at eight, so I might as well continue in my efforts to finish it off.

Help me next week, particularly on Tuesday.

May 27, 1991 — Memorial Day — Grand Beach

My Love,

I didn't make it up at four this morning to begin writing, and I ate too much yesterday, so my will power is falling apart, I fear. It's going to be hot today and hotter tomorrow — in the nineties and it's still May. But the rain continues.

I'm so tired today, the terrible rush and work of the past two months. Only ten more days and it will be over, save for the promotion tour.

I don't seem to be able to catch up. The more I accomplish, the more there is to be done. Obviously I put these obligations on myself and I don't know how to stop them.

Writing the novel — a task I usually love — has become a burden too. It wouldn't be by itself, but I have to squeeze it into a huge agenda of obligations. I think it can be done in the next two weeks, but I've come to hate it because it too has become an obligation.

So I dread this week — demands, heat, surgery, rushing around. Dear God, help me get through it and help me get back here and break out of this nonsense.

As I said yesterday, I have the feeling now (which I don't like in myself) of people draining life and time and strength away from me. No one ever calls to offer me help and strength.

I need to be left alone, I really do.

I continue to complain, for which I'm really sorry, but it's how I feel today, and You want me to tell You how I feel.

May 29, 1991 — Grand Beach

My Love,

I'm forging ahead on the novel. Six thousand words today. Before nine o'clock. I've reached that part of the story where I know exactly what will happen next and it just flows off the typewriter. I love it when that happens! I'll be glad when it's done just the same.

And thank You very much for the good news from the doctor! Grant that it may continue to be good.

I love You.

May 30, 1991 — Chicago

My Love,

I continue to make progress on the novel and to do so with ease, now that I'm on the 4:00 A.M. schedule. Only another week and a half's work I suspect. It would be so nice if I could go out in the country and do nothing but write — how many times have You heard me say that! However, being what I am and with all the commitments I have, that is not to be.

The amazing thing is how many people have told me recently that I look great, and that despite the pace I'm keeping and the hours at which I'm getting up. Moreover, while I feel very sleepy at the end of the day, I still sleep well at night, even last night when, because of the healing on my face, I didn't go swimming during the day.

So I'm in basic good health despite all the work, for which I am very grateful. Help me to survive the next difficult couple of weeks before I settle down at Grand Beach.

I love You.

June 2, 1991 — Chicago

My Love,

I didn't get up till six this morning. I simply couldn't keep up the four o'clock pace any longer. I'm not going to do anything today after I finish these reflections except work on the novel. I hope to have it finished by this evening. What a relief it always is to finish a story. If only there were some way to work on a novel without the distractions that beset my life and force me to get up early in the morning. If only storytelling could always be the fun that it is supposed to be. I must endeavor in the months and years ahead to rearrange things so that is what happens.

An image I encountered in my brief spiritual reading yesterday said that the self is the musical instrument and God is the musician. I am the new piano at the Chicago Symphony and You are Daniel Barenboim. I'm afraid I'm not a very tractable instrument these days, not at all. Help me.

And whatever happened to my prayer life during the day? Lost in Ireland, I fear. And done in by the novel.

Help me recapture it, please. I love You.

June 3, 1991 — Chicago

My Love,

The novel is finished, for which many, many thanks! I am very satisfied with it, indeed most satisfied. I think it is the best and most powerful story I've ever written and also has the strongest religious message. It came together quite well at the end. I wrote fifty thousand words in the last week, but there is no choice about that kind of effort when the story begins to converge.

Now I can settle down to enjoy the summer. Absolutely no sociology this time around. Just reading and relaxing and poetry. This summer there has to be poetry.

In my reading this morning there is much about aging and death, a subject about which it is necessary to reflect but not to brood. I don't believe that I'm sixty-three and I certainly don't act like it. But I am and for all my good health, for which by the way many thanks, my years are numbered. I must use them well, which does not necessarily mean working the way I have done the last couple of months.

Anyway, it's an enormous relief to have finished the book. I ask You to bless it and help it to have the impact on people that You want it to have.

I love You. Help me to get back to the regular routine of prayer with You.

June 7, 1991 — Grand Beach

My Love,

I'm back to regular spiritual reading, thank You, back to Sulivan, who warns us about being young again and traveling light and not being a servant to things. I'm afraid I'm very much a servant to things — three homes stretched out across a continent, computer and hi-fi equipment, the latter rarely if ever working right, too many clothes, too many cameras, too many books.

Can it be otherwise? I don't know right now, I'm so tired. Give me time, a few days to think about these things, to read, to begin to write poetry.

In Synder's poetry, which I'm reading now, he is very aware of his own mortality — and also of the love which makes it immortal. I want also to be aware of immortal love.

I love You. Help me in this time of exhaustion.

June 8, 1991 — Grand Beach

I've been reading Heiler's book on prayer, which is very interesting indeed. I note that he left Catholicism in Germany to become a Lutheran. Catholicism in Germany may not have been much in his era, but I wonder if he found much in the declining Protestantism of the same time.

Anyway, apart from the decisions of his own conscience, the book is excellent. His conclusion is that prayer is an attempt to find a deeper, richer, more intense life, a more blessed life as St. Augustine says, a life of depth, width, and significance.

How very true. I will revise my sociological report on prayer to include these quotes.

I also understand that my own life is richer and more blessed — by far — since I began this form of prayer on the computer screen, an idea for which I am indeed deeply grateful.

Now that I'm settling down (despite an intense day tomorrow in Chicago) I hope to improve my prayer, both the seriousness and the frequency of it.

"Hope to improve my prayer!" — What a fatuous phrase! But You know what I mean: explore deeply the richness of Your love for me, understand it better so that I can preach it and write better stories about You for others. I do love You.Help me to love You more.

June 9, 1991 — Grand Beach

My Love,

Reading Heiler persuades me that what I do here is prayer of the essence, the search for a blessed life along with a tremendous Lover. If only I could keep that search a little more in my mind during the rest of the hectic and chaotic days in which I live.

June 10, 1991 — Grand Beach

My Love,

I'm so, so, so tired. How weary You must be of that constant complaint from me! But I am really tired, as tired as I have ever been in all my life, so tired that when I came home last night I was too tired to sleep.

And at eleven when I had just got in, I received a call from Chicago. I must go back today for a wake. I need time to recoup, and I'm not able to get it.

I'm too tired even to pray. All I can do is throw my trust to You and beg You to take care of me and restore my strength.

I love You.

June 11, 1991 — Grand Beach

My Love,

A cool rainy day with a breeze coming in off the lake and the waves tapping against the beach. Somehow that seems just right after the heat and the humidity and the rush of the last couple of weeks. I have today and tomorrow before I have to go back to Chicago and begin the book tour. Not enough time to rest but better than nothing.

I continue to be so, so tired. And June is almost half over — destroyed by the foolishness I have imposed on myself.

Next year, should there be a next year, I will make a rule that I do nothing after June 1.

The woman whose wake I attended yesterday, a friend from the very beginning of my years at Christ the King, had written me a terrible note about my fiction, accusing me of writing porn to make money. She seemed to write me off and probably never changed her mind.

I paid little attention to her at the subsequent times at which our paths crossed. I shouldn't have done that. I write novels about forgiveness and don't forgive enough myself.

I suppose we will straighten it out together in the world to come. But I'm sorry about it, very sorry. You forgive me, even when I don't say I'm sorry. I should forgive others, at least to the point of being civil to them. I do not have to get into relationships with them that are close, but I still must forgive, while there's still time.

I love You. Be good to her, as I know You will.

June 12, 1991 — Grand Beach

My Love,

The sound of sea birds, the lake brushing against the beach, a fresh breeze, the roar of lawn mower, and a jet plane flying overhead — each in their own way a sacrament of Your presence lurking everywhere.

I read Talbot's book yesterday on quantum theory. Some of the ideas of contemporary science like "m-fields" and the "implicate reality" are fascinating and, I think, point in a direction that tells us more about the world in which we live and about those of us who live in it — and especially about You.

I recall my image of You as a teenage showoff. It is, as You know from my admiration of the vitality and hope of teens, a flattering image, but also an apt one because You certainly seem to have chosen elaborate, wonderful, and marvelous ways of doing things, a wisdom which would dazzle even the sages, a Lady Wisdom if there ever was one. Lady Wisdom as a teenager?

I like that irreverent image the more I ponder it. I wish this morning, as my vitality slowly returns, that I had the energy to be as playful in life as You are!

That's a dumb line, isn't it? How much energy does it take to play? The trouble is that so much of my energy is siphoned off for responsibilities and work that I am too enervated to play.

I want to play this summer in the worst way, but I must fight off the work and the responsibilities to do so, the erosion of play and prayer time by the demands of the world. I'll have to think that through and pray over it in the days to come.

This is my last full day at Grand Beach before I leave on the tour. I count five days that have been eroded one way or another before the tour by other demands. Protect me from them, I beg You.

I love You.

June 13, 1991 — Grand Beach

My Love,

I'm off again today on the first part of the tour.

And I am depressed again this morning, realizing how short my life will be, indeed how short life is, how much energy I've thrown into life, a lot of it for personal or neurotic reasons, I admit, and how little return there has been for the causes for which I've labored, and how much anger and animosity I've stirred up.

I'm tired and worn out, not only physically but even more emotionally and spiritually. So much rushing and I'm about to embark on another week of manic traveling. For what possible purpose?

I've been reading Hans Urs von Balthasar lately. Strange, learned, detached man. Like De Lubac, Daniélou, and Ratzinger, his work was at first condemned, implicitly or explicitly, in 1950. Later he became a cardinal, like the others, and seemed to betray the movements he helped to set in motion in the Church. If I have to choose between such men and the Metzes and Greinachers of the world, I guess I'll choose the former, but fortunately I don't have to choose.

But what does it all matter? I ask myself on this weary morning. Not even the victory of the Chicago Bulls last night cheers me up.

Take care of me and protect me during the trip.

I love You.

June 19, 1991 — Somewhere in America

My Love,

On the Metroliner to New York after seven interviews in the last twenty-four hours. A lecture tonight, three more interviews tomorrow, and then I can go home.

I'm so tired, tired beyond description, more tired than I have ever been.

I love You.

Help me to get through this time.

June 20, 1991 — Washington, D.C.

My Love,

I'm at the Four Seasons Hotel in Washington today, two interviews down and one more to go, plus lunch and supper. Summer begins late today, but the first day of summer is tomorrow and I'll celebrate it appropriately at Grand Beach.

The tour has gone well, good questions and no hostility. Whether it will sell books or not remains to be seen. The talk was received very well last night at the Smithsonian, which was nice. Slowly it dawns on me that the detractors don't bother to harass me anymore and that there is a large, dedicated, and enthusiastic group of supporters out there. The message from last night about You being Love in sociological perspectives really appeals to people.

The favorable mail continues to pour in. I must not let down this new parish You have given me. I must be loyal to the special vocation You have chosen for me and try to keep up the writing that will respond to what Your people want to hear about You — which is what I want to say.

Thank You for the opportunities and the ability to make the most of such opportunities. Help me to understand that I'm always a priest, no matter what happens.

(And help me to unwind back at the beach.)

I love You.

June 22, 1991 — Grand Beach

My Love,

Back at Grand Beach for the beginning of summer and the first day is cloudy and rainy so we can go skiing! Sure!

I'm still tired, desperately tired and also depressed, terribly depressed. I've done my spiritual reading this morning, and I believe that resurrection, or new life at any rate, follows death, but that message of hope does not overcome the physical weariness which assails me.

Help me to snap out of this slump. Grant me renewal and reflection this summer, I beg You.

June 23, 1991 — Grand Beach

My Love,

The sun is out again, and that picks up my spirits. I'm beginning to get into the summer flow again, but I have a long way to go before I settle in and settle down. I continue to be tired and discouraged and depressed. I did my spiritual reading this morning and nothing came of it except sadness about the passage of time and all the loss. I know that part of relaxing is contemplating the past and grieving about the loss. Yet I have so little to grieve about compared to others. I ought not to be melancholy but I am. Help me out of it, please.

I love You.

I will try to think of You often during the day today.

June 26, 1991 — Grand Beach

My Love,

I had a bad sinus headache yesterday and took some medicine to clear it up which in its turn made me sleepy. Yet my sleep was troubled during the night. I'm really in a bad way. Mary Kotecki said yesterday she had never seen me so tired.

I must go into Chicago tomorrow for an interview, prolonged into lunch and supper. It just goes on and on and on. How have I got myself into this grind? It's always about to end, but it never does. Three months of nightmare. I can't go on this way. Please help me!

And also help me to face the fact that I must help myself.

I love You.

June 28, 1991 — Grand Beach

My Love,

I left yesterday at 5:30 for Chicago and came back at 11:00 last night. The vacation which I have been striving for since June 1 keeps eluding me. I am so, so tired. I can't go on this way.

An article in *Theological Studies* described a theory of universal salvation that was consoling. I will have to reread it to make sure I can translate it into a pastoral speech, but I think it says that humans cannot definitively reject God. They can give only a temporary rejection since their "yes" to You is not of the same order as a "no."

Only the "yes" can be permanent.

I like that very much indeed. It fits the theology of the present novel perfectly. It makes creation a much more benign phenomenon. It also seems to respect Your love the way that You would want it respected. It also restores purgatory, not as a place of suffering, but as a place of growth. I hope so.

I love You.

July 1, 1991 — Grand Beach

The first of July and vacation begins. Already the burdens begin to lift.

And I begin to recall my dreams.

Last night I was back at Christ the King getting a haircut. I met Rich Daley on the street and walked back to the rectory with him. I had chewed the pastor out for being rude. He apologized, said he was sick the night before. In the meantime I talked to some sixth-graders who were in the rectory basement doing something for the parish.

The referents are clear — my love of parish, Grand Beach as my parish, my residual angers from the past, mitigated by understanding, the irony of my new position at Grand Beach, and perhaps some bitterness about the archdiocese.

No great revelation in those images, but their vividness shows me how much parish and neighborhood shape my religious imagination — and how much I miss Christ the King.

This last year the University of Chicago made its peace with me, the Church has not. Well, you win some and you lose some. I'm grateful for the win and I acknowledge as I have before that maybe the loss was good for me.

I love You. Thanks for the good beginning at last of this vacation and for the promise of more. Help me to enjoy it.

This afternoon to the beach!

July 2, 1991 — Grand Beach

My Love,

A spectacular storm dazzled Grand Beach last night. So much beauty in the world, proving that nature shows not Your existence but rather what You're like. I love You in all Your splendor, both the galaxies and the mites on the forest floor about which the *New York Times* wrote this morning. Every time I think of You, I'm dazzled, overwhelmed.

I don't know what You are other than a Lover but You are really something else, far more than any of our metaphors hint.

July 3, 1991 — Grand Beach

My Love,

My dreams last night were confused. I understood them when I woke up but lost them later. I must try tonight to use the tape recorder next to my bed.

But the dreams were about the parish or about parishes. No dreams are ever general. It was about a parish. Not Christ the King, not the real Christ the King in which I might not after all belong and might never have belonged really. But about a parish which symbolizes the importance of all parishes to me. I chose the two parishes as metaphor in my memoir because the parish and its life were critical in the development of my life, and I guess they are critical to my religious imagination too. They surely appear in all my novels in one form or another.

I grow angry at the total disregard for the parish and its worth by Catholic theologians and Church leaders. Maybe I'll try to write again about the parish this autumn and about marriage too, perhaps for *America*. It won't change anything in the Church but one must try.

Why do our elites, right and left alike, so condemn the neighborhood parish? I must continue to celebrate it. It is in the parish, however parochial it may be, that You manifest Yourself and Your love in the ordinary lives and loves of its people.

I must say that again and again and again.

July 4, 1991 — Grand Beach

My Love,

The fireworks last night were fun!

Thank You on this day for the freedom in our country. Grant that we may appreciate it more and that we might feel some sense of tragedy for all the deaths our country caused in Iraq.

I love You.

July 5, 1991 — Grand Beach

My Love,

My dream last night was a fierce one. I was a soldier, a swordsman and something of a coward, afraid to die in combat. The enemy stormed into the front door of the classroom we were defending with automatic weapons. I killed the leading enemy and then wiped out the rest with the automatic weapon I had taken from his painfully dying hands.

Good grief!

At one level it was a protest against the people who swarmed onto the beach in front of the house yesterday and drove off my nieces. At another, and more serious level, it's my own self-image of taking on the world, and especially the Church as I have done in my criticisms of the archdiocese and the cardinal. And me a coward at that, someone who does not like to fight or to alienate, but who, when I do, close in for the kill. Whew!

I must ask myself how much of this is anger and hate for what they have done to me. Criticism is essential, especially since perhaps they will eventually change. There should be more of it rather than less, but I must do it without hatred. So too with my struggle for truth about my stolen papers. I must do it in the name of truth and not of revenge.

I read *The Holographic Universe* yesterday. The various parts of the theory may not all be accurate. Surely it will be refined as time goes on. Yet it is an understanding of reality which is illuminating and explains much. The most important spiritual consequence is that it emphasizes the unity in love of everything. That I must applaud and reflect on as I hope to in the days ahead.

I love *You.*

July 6, 1991 — Grand Beach

My Love,

My guests will be here shortly. Everything is organized. I enjoy entertaining my friends. Help me to be a good host.

My dream last night was odd. I was a priest at the side of a hospital bed when a nurse turned off the life-support system of an aging woman (as in the news story yesterday).The woman seemed dead, so I didn't stop the nurse. Then the woman revived and I was blamed for attempted murder. Since I didn't stop the nurse, I was as guilty as she was. The dream was vivid and even when I woke I had a hard time persuading myself that I wasn't charged unfairly.

My stolen papers again, I guess — and the more generalized vulnerability I feel since I am on the margins and open to attack from anyone and everyone. Actually I haven't been attacked much lately, though there are a lot of folks who jump at the opportunity when it occurs, as some of the reviews show. The point I should remember is that I have survived through Your help and will continue to survive only with Your help.

Once more attention to my dreams tells me a lot about the state of my consciousness.

Well, I must run to finish my preparations for the guests. I'll return to the universe and You tomorrow or Tuesday.

I love You.

July 8, 1991 — Grand Beach

My Love,

Powerful dream last night about going back to Quigley to start my seminary days over — at my age. Then abandoning that as pointless, I return to Christ the King — to the Christian Family Movement and the Young Christian Students and High Club and eighth-grade teaching and defying the cardinal about my sociological work and freedom.

What does this dream mean? A longing for a youth that is lost? Surely that. Also, as in last night's dream about saying a funeral, a longing for parish and for being part of the archdiocese. But, even in the dreams, never an intent to compromise. When I wake up I realize that my life is so structured now that it would be impossible to return to parish work and that in St. Mary of the Woods I have a parish already, though not Christ the King.

How much that place has affected me! First love, I guess.

But I do not complain. Rather I understand myself a little better. For which, thanks.

Take care of me on the trip to Chicago today.

I love You.

July 11, 1991 — Grand Beach

My Love,

Here it is Thursday and I'm finally over the Monday trip to Chicago and a Tuesday stomachache. I am so grateful that, You being willing, I won't have to go back till Heidi's wedding at the end of August.

I read one of the two books that came out on the Henry Horner Homes [public housing] this summer. Chilling. The author, who is very angry, holds back his anger most of the time and eschews explanations or solutions. Yet the book has a slant of its own. I suppose, however, that if you have spent that much time in such a terrible place you can't help have a slant.

I thought often as I read it of Liz Moynihan's comment on Delhi, "not much different from London in 1750." The big difference of course is that in London in 1750, relatively few people were able to live different lives. In 1991, most people don't live in Henry Horner Homes.

Welfare is part of the problem. Public housing mistakes are another part of it. But neither can be undone. We don't know much more about how to deal with the truly disadvantaged than we did thirty years ago. Jobs, father-present families, decent education, are all part of the agenda, yet they are not enough.

So what can one do?

Minimally realize that You love those poor people as much as You love the teenagers here at Grand Beach. The kids here are not well-off because the people in Henry Horner are poor; guilt is not the solution (though I believe the author thinks it is). But what is?

I wish I knew.

In the meantime I pray that You enlighten all of us about what we should be doing.

July 12, 1991 — Grand Beach

My Love,

In last night's dream I was flying a B-17 from England to the States, not in 1944 but in the present, an old and reconditioned plane which was to appear in a museum somewhere. Only I had to fly it not from the cockpit but from the cabin (which was falling apart) and with a stick that didn't fit anywhere. They wouldn't let me in the cockpit and since we didn't have oxygen masks we couldn't fly high, and I would surely get motion sick over the Atlantic if I didn't freeze to death. Also, while I was responsible for flying the plane, I knew nothing about navigating or designing a flight plan!

I've had these airplane dreams before and these dreams of the impossible being demanded, but never the two of them together and never in a setting out of *Twelve O'Clock High!*

On the whole it was a pretty good metaphor for the impossible situations I find myself in, including Martin Charnin's invitation that I be a playwright. However, the metaphor goes beyond that. I am driven by a need to attempt the impossible and at the same time am afraid I can't pull off the risks I've taken.

I usually succeed, more or less, but the emotional strain is often great. It doesn't follow that I shouldn't keep trying. It only follows that I should realize what is going on.

Help me to continue to remember and understand these dreams.

The poems I'm reading are all about death and all depressing, though in both cases the authors are men of faith. It was almost a relief this morning to read St. Paul on resurrection. Oh, yes, indeed, St. Paul may often be irrelevant for our time. But when he is relevant, he is very powerful indeed. Help me to have resurrection faith that is a little like his.

Nice review of the published version of last year's reflections in the *Tablet*. I should read the book!

I love You!

July 13, 1991 — Grand Beach

My Love,

It's a cool, cloudy day, one of the few so far this summer. I decided against skiing and went back to bed and slept for two hours which was a very wise move. I continue to unwind and to feel much better. Summer, however, slips through my fingers all too quickly.

Sulivan says this morning that if one wishes to believe in God, one should not permit theological conceptualizations to get in the way. How right he is! Theology and concepts are essential: we must have them because we are thinking creatures and our thoughts need road maps, but once we have the map and know the schema of the territory, we've only begun to understand what the reality is like. Yet the temptation, particularly for the theologically obsessed, is to hide behind the road map and not risk oneself in the territory. Concepts are not relationships; they are not even metaphors, except in the most abstract sense of the word. They give us only the dimmest hints of what You are like.

For that we must turn to the world of metaphors, the language of the poets and of human love and of dreams. If it sounds like I'm on the verge of poetry, I guess I am. I grow increasingly dissatisfied with the poetry I'm reading these days. Unlike Heaney's it is devoid of religion. Can there be religionless poetry? Perhaps there can, though I'm not sure about that. But I don't think there can be great poetry without religion.

Anyway, I may just begin this afternoon or tomorrow to let the poet inside of me flourish again.

I missed the dreams last night, perhaps because I was so tired. I will try again tonight.

July 15, 1991 — Grand Beach

Just when I thought that I would never get anything out of St. Paul ever again, I come on the passages in 2 Corinthians about a new creation and realize how exciting those times must have been — the tremendous confidence that everything was new again, the whole of creation renewed.

What a long distance there is from that bubbling joy to the concept-ridden, power-obsessed Church of today on which Sulivan so mercilessly pounds in his book. A long way from 2 Corinthians.

It is the power obsession of the Church that destroys its appeal for so many people. The power obsession may be clothed in sacral robes and rationalized by the obsessed, but it is clear to everyone that the leaders of the Church are driven more by the need to protect their own power than by any other motive, whether the victim be Galileo or Hans Küng or, at a very lesser level, me.

When will reform ever come — not the reform which makes a perfect Church but merely the reform which makes a more humble Church? It's long overdue, my Love; You almost pulled it off with Pope John. Clearly You will have to try again.

In the meantime I must let myself exult in the sense of a New Creation and let that animate my own work.

July 16, 1991 — Grand Beach

My Love,

My dream last night was the parish reassignment dream again, to St. Ambrose, but a different St. Ambrose than the real one, though every bit as gloomy. As best I can figure out, it was a dream about my past fear of the archdiocese intervening to stop what I'm doing and reassign me. That fear as a conscious reality I left behind long ago. But it still lurks — excited again perhaps by my Galileo research and by the news clips on the awful pedophile cases I watched yesterday and which I feel must be exposed. It's a fear of the terrible authority structure of the Church on which it seems I have declared war, without intending to do so.

That fear must run pretty deep for it to keep appearing in dream metaphors. However, it doesn't bother me much consciously. I certainly don't pull any punches. I figure I'm too old to worry about pleasing the authority structure at this stage.

I must be careful, however, not to take it on out of pure contentiousness. I must at all costs avoid punitive or vengeful attitudes.

Help me to do so. I don't want to act out of hatred or anger.

July 17, 1991 — Grand Beach

My Love,

It's hot, more temperatures in the nineties. I can't complain about it being a bad summer, can I?

Sulivan complains this morning against those who substitute social action for the Gospel. I'm always amazed at how some clerics seek cheap grace by preaching on social problems that are beyond the scope of their people and ignore the fundaments of faith — all in the name of relevance! They mean "relevance" for themselves, not for their people.

I'm also astonished that my novels, which do preach of Your love for us, are thought to be a threat to the faithful, while the pedophile priests are not.

I guess I'm not in a particularly good mood this morning. And I don't really understand why.

Nonetheless I love You. Help me to love You more and to radiate that love and its accompanying joy in my life.

July 19, 1991 — Grand Beach

My Love,

I'm tired and depressed today, tired because I didn't sleep well last night after a day of entertaining guests and depressed because of the talk about the Church and the archdiocese which are all in a terrible mess. The young theologian who was here, however, is grounds for great encouragement. If You produce only a couple like him every generation, the Church will survive!

I'm not just now capable of much more, but I wanted to check in with You, tell You that I loved You, and report that I'll be back tomorrow with, I hope, better things to say.

I do love You.

July 20, 1991 — Grand Beach

My Love,

The young priest remarked the day before yesterday that attempts to distance You from creation (as in deism and similar theories like the argument that God is a force rather than a person) are in fact efforts to keep You at bay, to dispose of a God who is intimate with us. The Catholic imagination, however, linking You as it does in a *quaedem relatio* with Your creation, pictures You *lurking everywhere* — and how I like to use the word "lurk" because it pictures You as hiding with glee, ready to pounce on Your beloved.

Do I believe this picture? I truly do. Do I live my life as if I believe it? The best I can reply is that I do so sometimes. Mostly, however, I'm so busy running that I don't act as if I believe it.

Maybe if I believed fully and all the time that You were lurking everywhere in love, I would be less tired and depressed and less burdened by all the work I have to do.

Help me to continue to love You and to permit that love to grow and expand so it fills my life with peace and joy and serenity.

Please.

July 21, 1991 — Grand Beach

My Love,

Three weeks into my vacation and I'm afraid I'm depressed and weary. No real reason that I can think of except perhaps age and general discouragement about my work and the state of the Church and the heat and the gray day today. And end-of-weekend blues.

I've sustained myself for thirty-seven years in the priesthood by energy and dedication (let's leave aside for the moment the complex origins of both of these) and I now seem to be running out of both. I dread the demands of autumn just as I dread the end of summer. There seems to be no rest, no peace, no renewal.

Pretty grim, huh? I bet if I review the Sunday reflections of this year, I'll find that every Sunday I feel the same way.

"Dust," the great Aquinas said.

"Vanity of vanities and all is vanity," said Ecclesiastes.

Right now all I seem to want is to be left alone, uninterrupted by phones, doorbells, correspondence, invitations, and even guests — left alone with books and music and the beach, left alone from demands and schedules and obligations and chores — just left alone, that's all!

Like I say, pretty grim.

How long have I felt this way?

Just today? Or weeks, months, years?

I'm having a hard time remembering dreams again, but I do have impressions of trouble and concern, of isolation and the impossible. Some of my friends say I'm mellowing. In fact, I think it's the other way, that I'm growing more impatient and quicker to anger.

I don't like this reflection and I presume You don't like it either, though You like me anyway.

Help me to understand more clearly what my life is about and to trust more completely in You.

I love You.

July 22, 1991 — Grand Beach

My Love,

Not much change in my mood since yesterday. What is it?

A fear of death? Maybe. But that's not all. It's a sense of being without purpose or goal or excitement or anything at all to live for. *Weltschmerz?* World sickness? Didn't [sociologist] Pete Rossi once ask whether there had been any good news in the last thousand years? Has there?

The salt seems to have lost its savor.

My work, sociology or fiction, doesn't excite me now, but rather feels like something I do because I have to do it.

The vacation, to which I have looked forward for so long, is not fun, just more obligations and more food to eat.

At the party yesterday, a nice party with kind people, many of whom love me, I felt like an outsider. No, I must say more: I felt like a doomed outsider!

Doomed by what or to what?

Not to death but to... to loneliness? No. To failure? No. To weariness, exhaustion, to having spent all my forces?

I feel that I'm just going through the motions right now.

There is no sweetness left, not in my spiritual reading and not in my loves. Not even in You.

I am not saying that You're not sweet, but only that for one reason or another I cannot taste Your sweetness.

Dark night of the soul? I am not so deeply spiritual that I am capable of a dark night.

Burned out? But that's a cliché!

I must write a poem this afternoon. That might help.

Nonetheless I do assert, despite it all, that I love You and want to love You more. I thank You for loving me.

July 23, 1991 — Grand Beach

My Love,

A phone call this morning at 7:20! And yesterday in late afternoon an hour of calls, obligation calls that I had to make. People I wanted to talk to, of course, but still obligations. Vacation! Is there ever a vacation from the phone and the mail?

I'm complaining again. *I'm sorry*. Today will be another rushed day, perhaps with time on the beach, which is my salvation. Every day is a rushed day, even when I'm supposed to be relaxing. What am I to do about this? Should I give up all thought of rest and refreshment? Am I forever doomed to be racing the clock?

I am so battered and weary this morning, hardly able to function, yet I must go skiing and shopping and out for dinner and answering phone calls and entertaining guests. I'm so tired of it all. Will rest come only when I'm dead?

Help me to find moments of peace.

July 24, 1991 — Grand Beach

My Love,

I feel better this morning. I'm tired, but not depressed like I was the last two days. I wonder how much spiritual ennui is nothing more than a cranky metabolism.

I don't remember the dreams from last night, save that they were again all about doing the impossible in some fashion or the other. As best as I can calculate from looking back on my recent depression, it results from a combination of demands and responsibilities and the awareness that I am getting old. The responsibilities will increase, the demands will become more vociferous, and my capacities to respond will diminish.

And I'll never be given a chance to rest.

At the moment that seems to be what it was all about. An accumulation of hundreds of small things, really — letters and calls and obligations — but enough to blight a vacation and a life unless one learns how to cope with them.

Which, with Your help, I will do.

I do love You. You can claim to be anything You want, because I know who You really are!

"If I encountered God," Sulivan quotes a Buddhist monk in today's reading, "and He claimed He was perfect and all-powerful, I would hit Him over the head with a stick and throw the body to the dogs."

Well, that's pretty strong!

Of course, You have never on the record claimed to be either of these things. In fact, all You have ever claimed to be is Love.

The point in his quote is that we must not let concepts get in the way of You and our experience of You.

I would like to think that I love You sufficiently, that if I did encounter You I would be polite and courteous and sufficiently dazzled that I wouldn't care what You claimed to be because I was in love with You, and because I know who and what You are.

Except that I meet You all the time and I don't always act that way, though perhaps I am acting more that way now. Thank You for Your grace.

July 25, 1991 — Grand Beach

My Love,

I am reminded again how much I am a slave of the physical environment, an environment which in my hectic and hurried life I often hardly notice. Because I am the master of so much electronic gadgetry and can move rather quickly anywhere in the world, it is easy for me to forget that I am a body in place and subject to all the constraints of place. I defend the importance of place in my work and celebrate the places of my life but forget that I am anchored in space and affected by what happens there.

How passionately we humans forget our mortality, which is the ultimate measure of our bodily nature.

On the other hand, I live in beautiful places and often (indeed almost always) am insensitive to their beauty. Last night on my own I actually went out to watch the sun set over the lake, first time all summer. So many tasks, so many responsibilities in my life, and so little sensitivity to the beautiful world You built around me. I don't have time for it. There is so much to do, and I'm not supposed to be working this summer either! Help me to be at least a little bit more aware of the *place* in which You have put me.

Last night I dreamed again about the impossible, this time protecting the Church from a crazy priest, obviously a metaphor for the pedophile cases which preoccupied me for a part of yesterday. There seems to be no way out of the mess for the Church except public scandal and huge financial loss. If that is the only way the mess can be stopped, well, so be it, but what a terrible cost to have to pay.

I will receive no credit for being right about these problems or for forcing a solution through my columns. I'll only be more on the margins of the archdiocese. Well, so be it!

July 27, 1991 — Grand Beach

My Love,

Another weekend with guests so I'm rushing. Good people and I'm glad to have them and I'm grateful for Your sending them to me and blessing me with their love. But with guests there comes rush and responsibility, so You'll excuse me if I seem to be running. I love You. I thank You for the pleasant weather and these dear friends. Thank You for the pleasure of their company. And help me to continue to grow in my love for You and for them.

July 30, 1991 — Grand Beach

My Love,

Jack Shea sent me his new poem yesterday. When I called him to tell him that I liked it, I said it would be my spiritual reading for the rest of the week. I also read the two *New Yorker* pieces about Archbishop Rembert Weakland of Milwaukee. The poem and the article were a nice contrast for the day. The former is an outburst of the Catholic imagination that is dazzling. The latter is a grim and sad tale about the self-destruction of the Catholic institution. I must write Rembert, a good man.

The Shea poem is about Advent and John the Baptist and going into the cave to find the beloved child and discovering that the beloved child is the self. As I said to him, the mystic Meister Eckhart got in a lot of trouble for that kind of identification. Of course, the metaphor means (at the risk of injuring it by prose interpretation) that Your love for Jesus extends to us. To me. Or perhaps more precisely that the crib scene is a revelation of Your love for us. Rather than being the theological cause, Bethlehem is the metaphor, the revelation of a love for all Your children which has always existed. The cave doesn't *make* us the loved child, it *reveals* us as the loved child.

And Shea captured this beauty with his sore back and all!

Anyway, such a vision of what the faith is all about is a tremendous shot in the arm while I sit here worrying about the Church and the archdiocese and my own work and about getting old. All of these subjects deserve some concern. But they are not what really matters. What really matters is Your love and my role as the beloved child in the cave. Help me to keep that in mind during this day.

July 31, 1991 — Grand Beach

My Love,

I lent Shea's poem to Roland Murphy, who was here yesterday, so I'll have to postpone some of my reflections on it. Nonetheless, I remember a couple of lines: "We are ready for You like a cup for water, like a flute for breath." That doesn't describe me very well, does it? One thing I've never been in my life is docile to You. Oh, I've taken chances and run risks and crawled out on limbs, so in that respect I can perhaps be said to have listened to You. But I have not been serene, passive (in the good sense of that word), flexible, laid back, relaxed, whatever — waiting for Your breeze-like inspirations.

Quite the contrary, I have charged hard into reality as if what happens to me depends on my work and effort and not on Your guidance and love. I have not relied on Your love, not nearly enough.

A fair description of my behavior is that I act as if I think You might have forgotten about me or that You might be busy elsewhere, so I have to strive and strain till You have time to deal with me and my problems.

Obviously I must do my part, but I must also do so in confidence in the power of Your love. I have been too compulsive by far in trying to do it all myself. As a result I am often worn and weary, tired out and discouraged, harassed and hassled, depressed and discouraged.

It is getting late in life to change my ways. Moreover, some of the problem is the personality and character You bestowed on me and of which You must approve. Still I can acquire a little more patience and trust in whatever time is left to me. Roland said yesterday that last year was a year of good news for me. So it was. Mostly. But You don't see it in my behavior, do You?

Help me to become "ready for You like a cup for water, a flute for breath." Please!

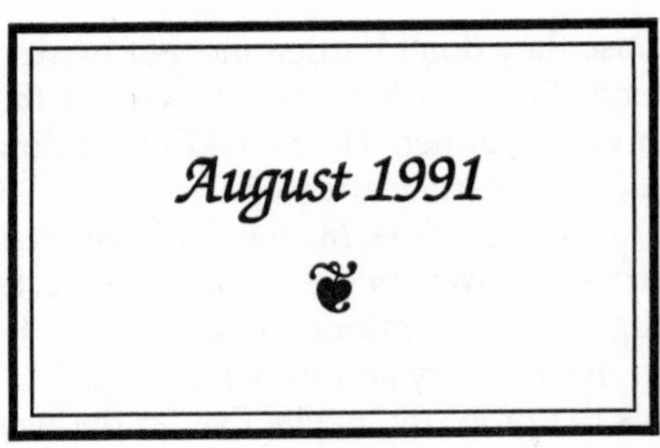

August 1991

August 1, 1991 — Grand Beach

My Love,

I reread Jack's poem this morning and was deeply moved by it once again. "Like a sentinel waiting for the dawn!" Exciting as the vision of the metaphor is, I find myself discouraged by it. Most of my life is over and I've wasted so much time, so much time. I ask myself where did I go wrong, what bad turn in the road did I take, how did I get myself out here where I am?

I am not talking about my career or my position in the Church; those were roads taken and decisions made which were valid ones and for which I need feel no regret. The Church is an institution of oppression, inflicting enormous injury on its people, and it is a good work to denounce this oppression. I mean rather my religious and spiritual choices, where did they go wrong? What happened to my spiritual life, my prayer life?

I suppose the answer (and I've in a way known it all along) is that I let the demands of the former, what I might broadly call my work, preempt my life. The contemplative got swept away by the active.

Yet I look at yesterday — a day filled up by phone calls and other duties. I didn't get to the beach until four. If I need to slow down to recapture the contemplative dimension of my life — and I have been striving to do that for years — how can I do it as long as there are so many outside demands that represent You too?

I don't know the answer to that question, I truly don't. Maybe it's my dessert as in the poem. Yet I feel so tied down, not by material goods because they don't burden me, but by responsibilities and commitments. Should I have made fewer of the latter and taken on fewer of the former? How could I turn down either of those two long calls yesterday afternoon?

I'm always racing with time. Maybe that's my dessert. Maybe the secret is to try to be aware of the dawn, the wine, the breath as I struggle through the final episodes in my life.

If only I weren't so weary and troubled.

Maybe that's the problem: maybe I've let the weariness and trouble get in the way.

I don't know. I've tried to reflect on this problem so often and I still don't even really know its terms.

Help me.

August 2, 1991 — Grand Beach

I'm running these days like I was back in Chicago and not on vacation. I think I must come to terms with the fact that this is my lot in life and that there never will be a time when I'm not rushing to keep up with my responsibilities. It's a rough way to live and perhaps one in which I will not live too long, but I don't see any way to stop it given who I am and what my life has come to be. If only I could remember You and Your love for me in the course of rushing around during the day.

There isn't any time these days to think. And I call it a vacation!

Please help me. *Please.*

August 3, 1991 — Grand Beach

I just celebrated the McHugh-Fox wedding out on the dune, shouting down the speedboat race, which roared all through it. I told the strawberry story, which as usual was great fun.

I believe in the image of You in the story (and I hope You laugh as we all do at it — no, I *know* You laugh as we do). The problem is that the imagery of the sacraments as metaphors of human love does not permeate my hurried, harried life as it should (Martin Charnin called about the play just as I was about to begin the service). Perhaps instead of feeling sad as I have through much of this week about my failures, I should have instead expressed gratitude to You for all Your help and especially for the wonderful images of Yourself You have given to me through nature, and the Church, and especially through Your son Jesus. I fear that most of the week I was lamenting my own failures in the great grace competition. I'm sorry.

Last night after the rehearsal dinner I went down to the beach to roll down one of the umbrellas. It was so lovely down there, hot, humid, lake rolling up on the beach, lightning ripping across the sky, the smell of summer and rain and moisture everywhere.

I wish I could go down there more in the morning and in the evening and absorb the wonders of Your presence.

I'll keep trying.

Now I'm off to the wedding reception. Take care of these two lovers in whose good lives You've let me play a part at various times and in various ways.

August 4, 1991 — Grand Beach

My Love,

Last night I dreamed about being in a hospital and going up to surgery and being afraid of the total loss of consciousness that comes from the anesthetic. As my sister Mary says, once you've experienced that, you dread ever facing it again because it seems like absolute nothingness. It is, I suppose, a fear of death. One hint of what death might be like, absolute nothingness.

I don't think that's what death is, and the data suggest that it isn't either. If it is, well, perhaps death itself isn't so bad, but dying is.

What led to the dream was reflecting on my friend Brian's condition at the hospital. Grant him life and health again, please. I'm not sure I'd have gone through that liver transplant surgery. The chances are so poor and life after it so dubious. Is it worth all the suffering? Well, we all must make that decision for ourselves, I guess.

I dread the thought of lingering in a hospital for weeks and months, like Dan Herr did last year, like poor Barb Daley too. I guess there's no good way of dying and I accept whatever form of death You have laid out for me, with the full acknowledgment that I am afraid of it, as my dream last night showed.

In the end all we have is You and our hope in Your love for us.

I have no choice but to commit myself to that love. Help me to live as though I am caught up in that love.

August 5, 1991 — Grand Beach

My Love,

I'm listening to Shea's latest tapes in the car, my "spiritual reading" for the week. This morning he speaks of the passage in Matthew where Your son complains that they would not fast with the Baptist or eat or drink with him. Excuses, always excuses.

I like to think that if I were around in his day I would have followed him, if only to listen to the stories. Did I not write to the rabbi the other day that both of us would have followed Jesus?

But what right do I have to think that I would? I am skeptical of all would-be prophets and gurus, indeed I am even put off by Shea's suggestion that Jesus was a guru. I don't want to be a guru and I don't want to have one.

Up to a point, this is a healthy attitude. Most gurus are false gurus and most prophets are false prophets. But would I be open to a real prophet? How would I know the difference? Would I not, if Jesus came down the road, act like those whom he challenged in the passage Jack quotes?

I don't know. I'd like to think I would, but I'm not all that sure. I suppose it is good and wise not to be sure. Maybe I'd better listen to Shea's tapes on Jesus as "spirit master" with a very keen ear.

Help me to be open to Your love.

August 8, 1991 — Grand Beach

My Love,

Shea's tape yesterday commented on the passage in which Your son invites us to come to him and he will give us rest. Jack emphasizes the tenderness of this passage in St. Matthew — Jesus' care and affection for those who follow him. The "rest" he gives is not, however, like the rest I seek sometimes — freedom from phone and mail. It's rather the complacent rest of the beloved in the presence of the tenderness of the Lover. You empty Yourself out in love for all of us. For me.

There was a time in life when I thought I was unlovable. I know now intellectually that an enormous number of people love me, both those who are close and those who know me only through my books. I am overwhelmed by a tremendous amount of love. For whatever reason (not enough explicit affection in childhood perhaps) I have not fully appreciated that love, permitted myself to enjoy it, to be swept along by it, to be soothed into Your son's rest by it. Even many of those who dislike me are more ambivalent than hating. They would like to be able to love me (as the man who said, inaccurately, the other day that I was a big factor in his life but he wasn't in my life). I realize intellectually the love and friendship in all these people, but I don't appreciate emotionally what it means, which may make my response to it less than it ought to be.

But then what about You, You who love me through all these human loves, You who reveal Yourself to me through all these human loves, You who lurk in all my human lovers? How little aware I am in my emotions, for all my intellectual assent, of Your love, Your emptying Yourself out for me.

I'm sorry. I think You understand why I am not quite set up to cope with being loved, at least to cope fully with it. But still I might be more responsive.

Help me to be more responsive. Help me to realize that when I say, "I love You," I am responding to immense love — love which truly bestows rest.

And thanks for the rain which has finally come to our parched land after six dry weeks.

August 9, 1991 — Grand Beach

My Love,

As I ask myself why I am not more conscious of being loved by You — to the point of Your emptying Yourself for me — and why I am not more conscious of the other many loves in my life — which in their own ways are forms of emptying too, I can think of two reasons. First, there are so many who act as if they hate me. And I tend to focus more on the animosity and ambivalence than

I do on the affection. Secondly, my work ethic, which drives me to schedule so much into each day of my life, does not give me time to be sensitive to the affection with which I am flooded. That is a terrible self-judgment and it may not be completely true, but there is enough truth in it for me to be horrified at the pace, the crowding, the rush of my life which crowds out everything else.

For example, I have guests coming today. I am glad of that. I look forward to seeing them. But hospitality will totally exhaust my day for the next three days, to say nothing of the week after next. I'll be literally run ragged.

Yet, and here's the puzzle: it is a return of friendship which moved me to invite these guests. And somehow in the midst of all the rush, I must try to remember that in welcoming them, I am welcoming You, that I am returning Your love as well as theirs, even if my degree of sensitivity to that truth is less than I would like it to be.

Anyway, grant that I may be more aware that my minor emptying is a response to Your total emptying of Yourself for me. I have so much to learn. Teach me.

August 10, 1991 — Grand Beach

My Love,

I'm on the run because I have guests and I want to go water-skiing since this will be the last week. I have been thinking the last couple of days about the near ecstasy (well not all *that* near) of the water-ski experience — wind, sun, and water against your face and body as you slide over the water. So much fun and so much sense of being one with nature. The same for pushing a small sailboat off the beach. It makes me wonder more what the Principle of it all is really like. Who are You who make the joy of water-skiing and boating and summer possible?

Why is there anything at all and why is so much of it so good?

Who and what is that which we call God?

Who and what are You?

And why?

Well, those are headache-producing reflections. The best answer is the most hopeful one, the one Jesus brought us — You are self-giving Love. I believe that and I believe that I encounter You, however transiently, on the lake.

Thank You for that grace.

I love You.

August 13, 1991 — Grand Beach

My Love,

Another lovely, lovely day. What a marvelous summer it has been! And for which many, many thanks. I was too tired yesterday from my weekend exertions to do poetry or to fully appreciate the beauty. Instead of the poem my imagination turned to the revision of one of the novels. I decided not to fight it.

Ace comes today, which is always a relaxing and fun day. So many friends for someone who didn't think people liked him! I suppose if I multiply that substantially, I get You. When I wrestle in my head with the question of purpose, I always come up with mystery and Mystery and the puzzle of what You're like. The biggest appeal of Catholicism is that it says You are more wonderful than other religions say You are; it does not make You so ineffable as to be totally unlike the glories of a day like today or the joy of human friendship or the Beauty of human beauty.

I love You. Help me to be more aware of Your beauty and Your glory and Your love!

August 15, 1991 — Grand Beach

My Love,

Today is the Feast of Mary in Summertime, a symbol of Your mother love for all of us. I distribute ice-cream bars to the kids after Mass as a simple symbol of Your love. As always, I wonder whether the kids get the point completely. Still if I ask them later, they do give a pretty good response.

Anyway the ice cream is good! Dove bars today, nothing but the best after Father Greeley's Mass!

The feast also celebrates the goodness of creation — of crops and vintage, of food and drink, of summer and warmth, of breast and womb. Both St. Paul and Sulivan insist this morning on the goodness of life despite all the evil. The mystery continues but goodness is not to be denied.

I pray for Jack Durkin, who is to have surgery (the sixth time!) for gall bladder on Monday, and for Jack Shea, who is still plagued by aches and pains in his feet. Please grant them recovery and health. Also Brian.

And I thank You for my health and renewed vitality and plead that it continue.

I do love You. I thank You for all Your wondrous blessings, especially ice cream!

August 18, 1991 — Grand Beach

My Love,

My guests from Ireland are here and it's a pleasure to have them, though I will be glad when this part of the summer is over.

If I am properly to enjoy these wonderful men as well as properly exercise hospitality, I must find relaxation time each day while they're here. Help me to do that.

Despite some darkly brooding days it has been a glorious summer so far, the best I can remember, for which I am very grateful, and also for the friends I have here. I'm sorry I haven't made the best possible use of it, and in particular that there's been no poetry. I shall keep trying on that. My need to write poetry is not too far from my need to breathe and eat.

On the other hand, those who haven't seen me in weeks or months and saw me yesterday tell me how great I look. I suspect that it's nothing more than a little sun. At least I don't look sick. Thanks!

I continue to love You.

August 23, 1991 — Grand Beach

My Love,

Friday and I haven't been on this screen to reflect with You for five days. I have however spoken to You at odd times during this week of hospitality, so You know that I'm still interested.

It has been a good if busy week, but how I regret the slow passing of summer. However, autumn is a time of resurrection after the death of Labor Day weekend, which I still slip and call Memorial Day because of my hunger for summer.

And soon I'll be eager to return to Chicago.

I'm off tomorrow for Heidi's wedding and the American Sociological Association meeting, so I may not be back to these reflections till Tuesday.

But I'll be in touch. Whether I'm aware of it or not!

August 28, 1991 — Grand Beach

My Love,

I'm tired from the last week and a half though less tired than I was yesterday. I should not have agreed to write those two papers. I knew how busy I was going to be. Yet how can I refuse a friend?

So much to do! The story of my life I'm afraid. I'm sorry.

August 29, 1991 — Grand Beach

I experienced a lot of war yesterday: reading a book about a Polish officer surviving in the underground and a concentration camp; watching Renoir's *The Grand Illusion* on video; and a play about war on HBO (the latter a gory offering of *Tales from the Crypt*). Then I consider what it means that 50 million people (at least) died during the war. I shudder at the individual deaths described in the book, at the fear and the suffering which preceded death, at the evil which took possession of the concentration-camp killers.

I can cope with those deaths only if I believe that You wiped away all the tears and gave more and greater life to the ones who suffered.

Did You?

If You are at all, then You did.

It's an old argument against You, this argument from evil, and in a sense it is a rotten argument because it leaves all else unexplained, but after a day looking into hell on earth, it seems a pretty powerful argument and one that won't go away.

Grant peace and rest and comfort and happiness to all who die terribly. We are so fragile. Protect us as best You can and bring us all home where we shall all laugh again and all be young again, this I beg You.

And help me to realize that I have very little to complain about.

September 1991

September 5, 1991 — Grand Beach

My Love,

There were some wonderful quotes in Sulivan yesterday about prayer: to pray is to introduce love, humor, and death into every action.

And: to pray is to confess that we are empty and that we are hungry.

Finally: we can attain our full human stature only by opening ourselves to the absolute.

There's enough in those three quotations to sustain me for a lot of reflections.

First, to pray is to introduce love into every action. This seems to fit my sociological paradigm that prayer is the template for our other relationships. If we can open ourselves up to God in prayer, we can also open ourselves to the other, whether it be the intimate other, the spouse, or the distant other, the criminal.

Presumably it works both ways: if we are open to the other, it will be easier for us to be open to God. It's impossible to sort out the direction of the causality, but it really doesn't matter. Intimacy with You and regard for the other correlate — not one to one. Prayer is an act of love, both flowing from and feeding human love.

Just as I often do not find time in life for prayer, I often don't find time for You. On the other hand, to the extent that I dialogue honestly with You I am open to love from others.

It's an empirical phenomenon, supported both by the data and by human experience — my own among others.

Therefore, my Love, I can see that the many failures of love in my life would have been less serious if I had been more open to Your love as experienced in prayer.

This is all logical and rational today. I'll become more involved emotionally, I think, as I continue to ponder Sulivan's words.

September 6, 1991 — Grand Beach

My Love,

Sulivan says that to pray involves humor. Well, that's a marvelous idea and I'm all for it though I never quite thought about it that way before.

In a scene in my novel two lovers end their act of love with laughter, the way all good sex should end. Lovers laugh. They laugh because of one another, because of the wonderful world that makes their love possible, because, like the Irish who made love in the fields during wakes, love defies death and that's a great joke (laughing in the face of death). If there is not laughter in an intimacy, it becomes heavy, burdensome, and dull. At my best moments, the love dialogue I try to carry on with You each day is comic — what could be more comic than a human addressing the Ground of Being as an intimate? It's a kind of blasphemy that I dare because You have called for it, and that is pretty humorous too.

I hope that the humor of my relationship with You never deteriorates into contemptuous familiarity. After all, You did start the Big Bang, which was a pretty neat trick. I don't think my "God Sonnets" do that. I hope I don't do it too often in these prayers. If I do, please attribute it to weariness. I know You love me even when I may be a little bit too casual with the One with whom I am dealing.

One ought never to be casual with lovers.

But one may laugh with them. If one laughs with God, one laughs with other lovers and vice versa. I asked Brian last night (and for his recovery, many, many thanks) whether he would rather image God as a tired old man or a bright young woman (which is the best image I have of You, though the tender, mature woman will do too). He laughed. No choice!

It's an image filled with humor. I know You don't mind it. Help me to continue to laugh with You.

September 8, 1991 — Grand Beach

My Love,

I'm sorry I waited so long today. I've been pressing ahead on the new mystery — wrote twelve thousand words today, which is not bad. Or maybe it's terribly bad if one thinks that such output is crazy.

On the other hand, it is the way I work best.

So You know as I work that I love You, no matter how distracted and weak my love may be. Just like last night I remembered my prayer at the end of the day when I'm almost too tired to keep my eyes open.

Not a great way to relate to a lover, is it? I'm sorry. I'll try to do better tomorrow.

Sometimes when I'm doing this reflection, I wonder whether You are really listening to me. Then I realize how stupid that is, because if You're not there to listen, how come I exist at all?

I promise You that at 8:45 tomorrow morning, I'll be here wide awake — after five hours of work — and ready to talk to You in a more composed fashion.

I *do* love You.

September 10, 1991 — Grand Beach

My Love,

As I promised, I'm back at only two minutes after 8:45, now with nineteen thousand words of the mystery written, a third done by the end of the day.

It's fun again because as in most of my mysteries I don't know any more than the reader does who the criminals are at the present state. I only know that the heroine isn't one of them.

I don't even feel particularly exhausted. Big rain last night and lots of leaves on the ground. Summer is winding down. As You know, when that happens I get anxious to return to Chicago. But unless the weather turns completely sour, which doesn't seem likely, I plan to stay till the end of September, maybe with a quiet week at the end.

Also I did work the bit from yesterday's reflection into the story.

To pray, says Sulivan, is to confess that we are empty and hungry.

Oh, boy! I know what it's like to be hungry and empty, because I feel that way now with my attempt to lose the excess summer weight. Is that the way I feel spiritually? Is that why I try to talk to You this way every day? Is my life one of emptiness and hunger?

Not consciously so most of the time. I'm too busy to be aware of it all the time. But when I slow down and think for a few moments, as I did last night on the beach before I went to bed, I realize that there is something missing in my life, that there will always be something missing. I suppose that's another proof that there is an Absolute (You). Why else would we have a hunger for the absolute?

So yes, I am hungry and empty. I need to pray. This format is, if You will, a "starter," but one that has worked pretty well. Sometimes I do it because it's an obligation, one more responsibility in a life full of responsibilities, but I like to do it too. It's a big help in my life. It does help to fill some of my hunger and emptiness. For which, many thanks.

And I'm going to put the quote from Sulivan on Blackie's lips today!

I love You!

September 11, 1991 — Grand Beach

My Love,

Two good quotes from Sulivan this morning, one in its turn a quote from Eckhart: "Some people believe in God the way they believe in their cow — because it gives them butter and eggs." The second is pure Sulivan: "I am bored with a God who created for His own glory." The Gospel, he adds, is not concerned about how God created; catechism is!

He is warning us that we are so easily trapped in language. We really believe that the how and why of creation, which has caused so much Christian agony in the evolution issue and so much embarrassment to us in the Galileo case, is important compared to what Jesus came to tell us about You.

That's pretty stupid, come to think of it — another case of Christianity letting others define the issue for us. The Gospel doesn't picture You interested in self-glorification. It pictures You as a Lover. The glory bit may be sound like it's from a catechism, but it is lousy religion.

I didn't like the honor and glory of God when I heard it in grammar school fifty-seven years ago. I wonder whether it has ever been anything more than words to repeat?

Well, we're mostly out of that now, I hope.

But we have not even begun to understand what it means to picture You as a lover.

I *know* that's what You are. It is with a lover that I try to do these dialogues, but I still have a long way to go. Please help me to travel down that road.

September 12, 1991 — Grand Beach

My Love,

Sulivan today celebrates the work of poets and storytellers. His theory is in French terms and mine is an American sociological perspective, but our theory is the same — the Gospel is poetry, and religion is passed on by image and story. I sometimes am discouraged that so many Catholic intellectuals and priests don't seem to comprehend this. The reasons, I suspect, are that I'm a priest and that I make money and that prevents the theme and the message from being heard or read. The readers know but the people who could bring more readers don't.

Well, there's nothing to do about that, but it's a shame. Priest writes steamy novels is the image and I guess we can never kill that. Though it constantly astonishes me, because of course the novels are not steamy and wouldn't be considered steamy if anyone else wrote them. There is a curious image of the priesthood and a curious theology of the priesthood lurking behind the image. Probably it's our own fault for pretending not to be part of the human race.

The other charge, from the hierarchy, is that they are "inappropriate" for a priest and that some laity are shocked. They'd be shocked by the Song of Songs too, which is surely "inappropriate" for the Bible. But those arguments don't work either, not for those who are of a mind to condemn or oppose. I am angry every time I hear about another pedophile scandal in Chicago and think of the cardinal's protest that my books shock.

Oh, well, I had to get that off my chest. It's been a hard day at the screen — electricity went out and I had to sleep for an hour because of extreme weariness.

Tomorrow I will be back with more reflections on Sulivan and the role of the storyteller and my responsibilities as a storyteller.

September 13, 1991 — Grand Beach

My Love,

I finally did something sensible. I turned off the phone till one o'clock. That gave me from four to one to write, nine uninterrupted hours. I felt pretty tired at the end, though now after a swim and some reading and some time on the beach gazing at the sunset, I feel great.

Why have I been so reluctant to turn off the phone? I'll be darned if I know. The excuse is that maybe something important will come through. But what is so important that it can't wait till one?

Now to Sulivan on storytelling: I understand how important it is, the most important thing we can do and surely the most significant thing I do. I know at least intellectually how much impact my stories have. I wonder whether I respect this gift (discovered late in life) enough.

An incredible gift — which I didn't even know I had till I was over fifty.

Yet I use it at breakneck speed. The religious possibility (new life, beginning again, death and rebirth, peacemaking) is locked into every story, probably because I am a person whose head is dense with religious imagery. So the religious content is clear. To make it doubly so, I have Blackie Ryan and others preach almost outrageously.

But can you write a good novel as quickly as I do? I think you can write a good mystery with interesting characters and a tender love story in a short time. A great novel, no. But who writes great novels? So-called serious novels are another matter. Should I try to write a serious novel or should I stick to what I do well and what people find helpful?

The problem is that I often feel kind of cheap when a book is finished because I have done it so quickly, not with little effort because I work very hard, but still so easily. How can it be really good?

This is something I must reflect on in days ahead, a touchy point that must be touched.

Help me to probe it.

I love You.

September 14, 1991 — Grand Beach

My Love,

I decided when I woke up at four this morning that I would take today off and so I went back to sleep. It was the sensible thing to do and I should have thought of it last night. I'll stay an extra day at the end of week after next to make sure that my mini-vacation is full.

Now about my stories and my own feeling that they're not very good, a feeling that is to some extent reenforced by some of the people who don't like them. The serious pop culture critics ought to have convinced me by now that they are good and will last no matter what some of the papers may say. I am not so much affected by those who say you can't write as much as I do and expect it to be good.

If they do affect me at all, the reason is that I lack the confidence myself. No, the real reason is that I can't believe inside me that something I have done at almost reckless speed can be very worthwhile. I do it that way because someone wants it done, a contract in some cases, and so I do it quickly to honor a commitment.

Hence, I think, it isn't very good.

Despite what all the readers say.

So I don't read my own books.

I admit that's strange.

I don't have any novel to do now until almost two summers from now — lots of time, should You grant me that time, to reflect on how to proceed. Grant me wisdom.

I love You.

September 15, 1991 — Grand Beach

My Love,

I went to Chicago today for a Bear game, Don't ask me why when I could just as well watch it on TV. I suppose it was because I wanted to see Jack Shea and he's not yet ready to sit through a whole game, with his bad back.

I watched the film *Stop the Church!* the day before yesterday. It was pretty terrible. The gay group Act Up turned the Church into an inkblot for all their anger. But Cardinal O'Connor gave them some grounds to do so. The twisted ecclesiastical politics which put him in New York and Cardinal Law in Boston and Cardinal Bevilacqua in Philadelphia are scandalous. Nothing like giving You something to shout at.

Appointments like these, to say nothing of some of those that are even worse, are all designed by the pope's explicit plan to restore the power of the institution and especially its center over the lives of the people, particularly their sexual lives and their married sexual lives. Indeed this attempted restoration of power is close to idolatry because it makes the institution more important than its members.

Ugly and evil. Perhaps it teaches us how little faith we should put in our institutional leaders and how little we should listen to them. It is necessary, I guess, to demythologize the leadership. They are doing it for us and with a vengeance.

Yet we need leaders. Please grant us better leaders and give strength and courage to those who lead us now!

Is there any more I can do besides mixing loyalty and criticism the way I do now? I'm not sure but probably not. I must think about this. Grant me wisdom.

I love You.

September 19, 1991 — Grand Beach

My Love,

I feel stronger today than I have in a while, but concerned about a friend's misfortune I learned of yesterday and about all the failures and troubles and tragedies of the human condition — about victims of war and poverty and disease. Granted that we are often the creators of our own problems (though some things like sickness are not our doing), it still ought not to be that way.

We are such limited beings not only in our physical realities but also in our personalities — so much the prisoners of the past, of our rearing, of our biographies, of our physical conditions. Free, yes, but also constrained.

I know that from my own personal experience, and I see it so often in others. In my case it has not meant tragedy. For so many of my friends it has.

Help them, I beg You. And help me too.

I love You!.

Thank You for Your unconditional love!

Appendix: How Just a War?

I begin by saying that I believe the war in the Persian Gulf was immoral.

It was a cheap and easy victory in the number of American casualties. Our military performed brilliantly, better than it has any time since Patton and Bradley swept across France in the summer of 1944. The Iraqi power to wage war was destroyed, perhaps permanently. Kuwait was liberated. The danger of future aggression in the Persian Gulf was diminished, if not eliminated completely.

What more could one ask for from a quick and glorious little war?

Americans are proud of this swift, painless triumph. They rallied behind the "troops"; they displayed yellow ribbons and the flag; they ended the "Vietnam Syndrome." The Democrats who dared to vote against the war in the Senate are political outcasts. Everyone feels good about America again.

The popularity of a war, however, and the ease of victory do not make the war just or moral. The Persian Gulf war is popular precisely because the victory was so quick and the casualties so few. If it had continued for another month or two, and a thousand or ten thousand Americans had died, it would quickly have become an unpopular and immoral war with the American people—"another Vietnam."

Reprinted by permission of *The Critic* magazine.

Thus, there is one criterion and one alone, it would seem, in the United States for a just war — a minimum of American casualties.

As *one* criterion, I will not reject it. It fits neatly under the traditional just-war rubric that the good accomplished must outweigh the harm done. But as the sole criterion, it is profoundly immoral because it enables a people to ignore the deaths of other human beings, tens of thousands in this war, perhaps hundreds of thousands when the final count is made.

We killed those Iraqi soldiers and civilians — our army, our air force, our navy, our "smart bombs," our political leadership, our people by their overwhelming support for the war. We knocked out their industry, their communications, their electric power. We shoved them back into the preindustrial age; we exposed them to the risk of disease and famine; we looked on while the Kurds, who rose in rebellion at our urging, were slaughtered by the Republican Guard that our president permitted to escape from the trap the American military had sprung on them. We came to the aid of the Kurds reluctantly, and only after the Europeans shamed us into it. The reluctance was not limited to our vacillating president; the American people did not want to help the Kurds either, save perhaps to set up camps in which they can languish for another generation or two.

The American government and military, with the consent of the American people, killed tens of thousands of human beings, broke the hearts of many tens of thousands more (mothers and fathers, sons and daughters, sisters and brothers, wives and husbands), and caused an enormous amount of human suffering.

For the record, we couldn't care less about this suffering so long as "our troops" come home safely. For the first time in my life, I am ashamed to be an American.

It seems almost irrelevant to question why we worked this enormous havoc on so many innocent people.

It was not blood for oil because we did nicely without the oil of Iraq and Kuwait. It was not because the Iraqi takeover was unjust. We don't fight wars against other forms of injustice in the world — the oppression of the Palestinians on the West Bank and in Gaza, of the Tibetans, of the Timorese, of the Lithuanians and the Armenians and, especially, as it turns out, of the Kurds. Why was Kuwait so important? Because of the military threat of Saddam Hussein?

Clearly, he was a paper tiger. American tanks destroyed four thousand Iraqi tanks to the loss of four of our own. This is not war, it's massacre. The Sioux Indians did much better against the American Army than did the Iraqis. We killed more of our own than they did. The Scud missiles proved ineffective save for keeping people awake at night. Our Cruise missiles knocked out Iraq's chemical, biological, and nuclear capabilities in the first two nights of the war. The strength of Iraq's army was greatly overestimated — deliberately so, I fear. We were told that there were over a half-million Iraqi troops in Kuwait. It turns out that this was three hundred thousand more than were actually there. That is not an intelligence mistake. It is a deliberate lie.

If it were ever necessary to eliminate Iraq's military threat, such as it was, Israel could probably have done it in a couple of days. Or we could have moved our Cruise missile ships into the Gulf and done it ourselves.

If the war was not necessary because the Iraqi military threat was in fact nonexistent, what reason remains? To drive Saddam Hussein out of Kuwait — and thus return the barbarous Sabeh family to power and permit the Kuwaitis to murder Palestinians the way the Iraqis murdered them?

Surely, the sanctions would have accomplished the "liberation" of Kuwait eventually. If we were deliberately deceived, as I suspect, about the strength of Iraq, we were almost certainly deceived about the sanctions "not working." Postwar revelations indicate that the military leadership, Powell and Schwartzkopf, thought that sanctions would work and that a war was unnecessary. CIA Director William Webster testified to Congress that the sanctions were working, then reversed himself under administration pressure — though not quickly enough to save his job. It would appear that President Bush's concerns were "political." It did not matter whether the sanctions were working; he thought that he needed a quick end to the crisis. The trouble with the sanctions, from the president's point of view, was not that they were ineffective but that they would take "too long."

What was the rush? Hundreds of thousands of people would not have been killed and hundreds of thousands more lives would not have been blighted if the United States had been more patient. Somehow, Mr. Bush seemed to think that patience would have been a sign of weakness. In fact, impatience is the behavior of weak men and weak countries.

There was no sound reason for the air war. If there were such a reason, the first few nights would clearly have sufficed. *A fortiori*, there was no good reason for the ground war. In fact, there was no ground war. What happened was an occupation of territory that was ours for the taking. Anyone can be a brilliant strategist when the enemy is a fifth-rate power that has already been beaten.

Again, I ask, what was the rush? As far as I can see, the only reason for the rush was President Bush's vindictive personal feud with Saddam Hussein, just as the reason for our invasion of Panama was his personal animosity toward Manuel Noriega. Mr. Bush wanted to prove that the United States was the strongest military power in the world and that he was not a wimp. If there are other reasons for the war, they escape me.

Then, in his betrayal of the Kurds, Mr. Bush proved that he was a wimp after all and that the most powerful military nation in the world could do nothing to help a people who had risen in defense of their freedom at our instigation.

Moreover, Saddam Hussein remains in power, no collective security pact has been established in the Gulf region, and peace is no closer between the Arabs and the Jews. None of the strategic goals of the war have been achieved other than the destruction of the Iraqi military and the devastation of that country — goals which were hardly necessary, as it turns out, for the self-interest of the United States.

It was an unnecessary, useless, senseless, evil war. In a just world, Mr. Bush and Mr. Cheney, as well as Saddam Hussein, would be tried as war criminals because they were responsible for the deaths of so many innocent people without sufficient justifying reason. I am convinced that history will judge Bush and Cheney and their advisers as war criminals and the American people, with all their flags and yellow ribbons, as guilty of complicity in war crimes.

It will do no good to blame Saddam Hussein for the deaths. We killed them, he didn't; and we could clearly have triumphed over him one way or another without killing so many human beings. In terms of the just-war tradition, I deem the war to be immoral not because the cause was unjust but because all peaceful means had not been exhausted, because the force was disproportionate, and because more harm was done than good accomplished.

The American leadership seemed completely unaware of the

age-old truth that the effects of war are utterly unpredictable and that war should be postponed till no other response is possible. I don't suppose an anticipation of the Kurdish tragedy would have persuaded the president to moderate the demands of his macho ego; but it might have made clear to Americans that no war is cheap or easy — at least those Americans who believe that an Iraqi life or a Kurdish life is as valuable as an American life.

Having thus condemned the war in the strongest possible terms, I come to the basic thesis of this article: I may be wrong. I don't think I am wrong, but I could be. I sound certain, as everyone must in an argument about morality, but honesty compels me to admit that, in a complicated world like the one in which we live, no one can be completely certain about most moral issues.

Not even Cardinal John O'Connor.

There has been criticism of the just-war theory in *America* and the *National Catholic Reporter*, for example, on the grounds that it "has no teeth" and that the American bishops were not vigorous enough in condemning the war in terms of that theory. Such complaints would turn the just-war theory into a two-by-four with which the Church and its leaders can beat the government and its leaders and the people over the head.

Most religious leaders and especially most Catholic leaders expressed grave reservations about the war. Catholics in the United States Senate were more likely to vote against the war than Protestants. Moreover, if the media had cross-tabulated surveys by religion, I'm sure Catholics would have been more likely to oppose the war than Protestants. What more can one expect from the impact of positions taken by religious leaders, especially when the reason for opposition to the war is not that the cause is unjust, but substantially more subtle, that the means are disproportionate?

The critics of the just-war theory want that theory reduced to a simple paradigm which can quickly and instantly be applied to every situation and thus force everyone to accept the position that the critics hold.

Why don't you bishops, the implicit argument runs, force everyone to agree with us?

When is the Catholic Church, it was asked back in the 1960s, going to insist that America get out of Vietnam? The question was meant for the leaders of the Catholic Church. Now the question is asked in a similar fashion: Why didn't the Catholic Church condemn more vigorously the Persian Gulf war?

I submit that the question is totally inappropriate and that it indeed accepts the anti-Catholic model of bishops giving orders and laity submitting to those orders. Many "liberals" on the left wing of the Catholic population are quite at ease with this model so long as the orders of the bishops support the liberal/left party line.

I preached on two Sundays about the war, laying out quite carefully the just-war theory. But I did not apply it to the Persian Gulf war. As I told my congregation, they could read my columns or talk to me personally if they wanted my opinion, but I would not insult their intelligence or abuse the pulpit to try to impose my opinions on them. It was their job, not mine, to apply those principles to the practical situation. What did I know that they didn't which enabled me to insist that they agree with my application of principles to gray, complex, and problematic reality?

I submit that, in most situations, this is all religious leadership can or should do. In the modern world, Catholics must make their own decisions on highly problematic and contingent political situations. They will anyhow and, since they are quite capable of making moral decisions by themselves, they should.

That wouldn't stop the war, comes the reply. But this is an arrogant reply. What right does religious leadership have to think it can stop a war by itself? What right does the ideological left have to think that it can do so by the purity of its motivations and the brilliance of its reasoning?

You make your argument, you do what you can. Beyond that you cannot force your opinions on others. In a free society you persuade, you don't impose. In fact, as during the Vietnam conflict, when you try to impose by demonstrations, you win converts to the other side.

Are issues never so clear that one is dispensed from thinking one might well be wrong? Must one always concede to the other side of the argument that they might be right? Must one always acknowledge that matters are so obscure, so problematic, so confused that men and women of good faith and good will and good judgment can responsibly and morally be on both sides?

I reply, with the same wariness about the grayness of reality which I hope characterizes this article, sometimes.

This is an apparently weak answer; it is an answer that will infuriate those who want vehement condemnations. I'm sorry, but I think it is the only honest answer.

Should the Church, to illustrate by an example which will bother few readers of this article, be on the side of the breakup of Czechoslovakia or its continued union? Dear God in Heaven! Who knows?

To be somewhat more pertinent, should the Church support free trade in Eastern Europe although it will mean economic hardship for many people — at least in the short run — on the grounds that it is the only way that long-term prosperity can be attained?

Again, who knows? A meeting of bishops or moral theologians or liberation theologians? Gimme a break!

Bishops, priests, and laity can be on either side of the question and argue the morality of their position with passion and vigor, but do not invoke Jesus or the Church or a monopoly on moral concern to support your position.

Again, this will seem a weak answer. It is, however, the only appropriate answer in our complex world.

Those who want "teeth" in the just-war theory want a simple world in which there are no hues of gray. Sorry, but that's not the way things work.

"What about Hitler," comes the answer?

At one level, the question doesn't seem worth answering. It is impossible to dialogue with those who do not see the difference between the Persian Gulf (and Vietnam) on the one hand and Nazi Germany on the other. The comparison is obscene and one ought not to argue with obscenity.

It must be said, however, that if the United States was engaging in a war in which the cause itself was wrong (as the Mexican-American war may have been), then matters might be much simpler. Thus, if we invaded western Canada because we wanted to take over their tar sands, for example, the moral judgments would be much simpler. Or, if we herded all the Italians in the country into concentration camps because they were "inherently criminal" (as the National Immigration Commission directed by Congressman Dillingham said at the turn of the century), then the moral issue would be pretty clear.

Or, to deal with an issue that is real today, the treatment of Mexican-American immigrants is evil in itself. I will not admit that those who approve the present policy might be right. I deplore as patently and inexcusably sinful the cruelty to "illegals."

And, for the record, I applaud concern for the spotted owl.

The Persian Gulf war, however, was immoral because we did not exhaust peaceful solutions, because the means were disproportionate, and because the harm done outweighed the good that might be expected. When one tries to apply these components of the just-war theory, clear and certain moral solutions are simply not possible. One can passionately disagree and still admit that one might be wrong.

It is a moral humility that religious leaders and ideologues of both right and left find hard to practice. When ideology and religion are combined, such humility becomes even more difficult.

In a complex world and in a civil and pluralistic society, however, there does not seem to be a reasonable alternative to moral humility.